# Internal Alchemy
*A New Perspective*

© 2015
Classical Chinese Medicine Society
Forres, Moray, Scotland, UK

# Internal Alchemy
*A New Perspective*

By Dr. Bisong Guo

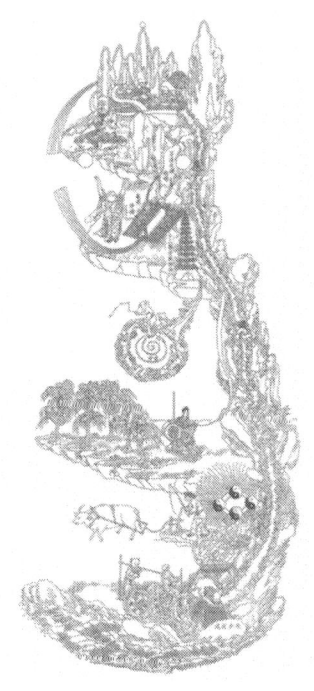

# Dedication

I would like to express deep gratitude to my divine teachers, who have revealed to me the wisdom and truth of the cosmos. With their guidance, I have come to understand that all living creatures have Buddha nature and that it only requires freedom from the ties of the ego for this true nature of the self to become manifest.

# Acknowledgments

I would like to express my sincere thanks to Kate Chen for her initial translation of the manuscript from Chinese to English, as well as to Martin Forbes and Kelda Spratt for proofreading and their editorial assistance. Lastly I would also like to thank Rob Veater and Mingming Poon for their administrative support.

# Contents

Preface ..... 11
Introduction ..... 15

## Part One
### Chapter One
Internal Alchemy for Immortality ..... 29

### Chapter Two
Heaven, Earth and Human as One – The Password of Our Civilisation ..... 43

### Chapter Three
External Alchemy – One of the Forerunners of Modern Science and Technology ..... 55

## Part Two
### Chapter Four
The Earth Cauldron and the Fate of Men ..... 65

**Chapter Five**
Why Doctors of Chinese Medicine Must Be Able to
Connect With the Divine                                        77

**Chapter Six**
An Overview of Daoist Internal Alchemy                         91

# Part Three
**Chapter Seven**
Modern Internal Alchemy – Wakening People through
Intensive Practices                                            123

**Chapter Eight**
Couples Practice, Solitary Practice, Early Practice            139

**Chapter Nine**
Internal Alchemy – The Effective 'Medicine' That Gives
Human Beings New Hope                                          151


**Appendix A-** Western Alchemy                                157
**Appendix B –** Mountain Skills in Nine Parts                 169

**About the Author**                                           175

# Preface

Over the past thirty years or so I have practiced Chinese Medicine, taught Qi Gong and classical Chinese philosophy alongside practices for healthy living in the UK, Continental Europe, China, Australia and North America. Wherever I've been I have quite often stayed with a local host who has helped organize the treatment sessions and teaching/training retreats. These experiences have allowed me not only to encounter, but also to develop a familiarity with, extremely special groups of Westerners. Despite being brought up in the West, they are intrigued by the culture and traditions of the East. Moreover, they are very serious about their spiritual refinement and practices. Some of them have taken spiritual journeys to India in order to participate in various spiritual practices.

Within this group of friends and students are scientists, teachers, medical doctors, psychologists, engineers and technicians, to name just a few. Some even have European royal blood or aristocratic titles. The majority of them are practitioners and students of Chinese Medicine, or of other natural and alternative practices.

I have learned so much from these very special individuals. For example, I have been introduced to areas of knowledge such as the Mayan calendar and western astrology and their interpretation of connections between the celestial order and human society, and how energy can be generated through the connection between heavens and Earth. To offer two examples - the Forbidden City in Beijing was built in accordance with the Ursa

Minor/Zi Wei constellation while Washington DC was apparently built to correspond with the Virgo constellation. It is believed that correspondence with the twelve different star constellations of the zodiac can allow humans to channel and obtain heavenly energy and power.

My friends and students have also shown me how church sites in ancient Europe were selected based on the meridian structure of the Earth; pointed church spires are like acupuncture needles linking the Earth with the energy field of the cosmos thus regulating the meridian balance of the Earth. I also learned about the method of daily practices of the seven chakras within the Indian tradition; that the shape of the pyramid is the basic structure of universal energy (the structure shared by the ancient Egyptians' royal tombs); the lotus meditation posture, and the structure of quarks, to name just a few.

I have also learned that there are twelve star gates on Earth which are pathways that lead to celestial and extra-terrestrial civilisations and that one of these gates is located at Xi'an in China. Traces of information/evidence regarding these celestial and extra-terrestrial civilisations can be found in these areas.

Human beings are the universe's experiment of free will and self-supervision. Our only pathway to enter the higher orders of the universe is through internal alchemy practices, where our energy fields will be able to turn into golden and pure white lights. Human civilisation is inseparable from extra-terrestrial civilisations. Some people have told me quite openly that their spiritual selves have experienced astral travel. Others firmly believe that they are beings from other planets reincarnated into human form. These people are indeed very sensitive to the energy field of Qi. Some can even read others minds. Some love the Ancient Chinese text the *Yi Jing* (*Book of Changes*) and use it for guidance. They all are extremely interested in Daoist practices, and the *Dao De Jing*, believing that the 'Heaven & Earth correspondence' principle is the primary foundation of human civilisation. They love nature and at the same time have a strong desire to practice internal alchemy.

We have talked about soul and spirituality, energy fields, time and space transformation, miracles, religion, culture, economics and so on and so forth. On occasion, we have created a Dao magnet (a dowser) - a simple method that helps to detect a local magnetic line. Overall, and most importantly, within this very special circle of international friends, we have shared our deep concerns for the fate of humanity, as well as the current state and future destination of our spirituality. These spiritual dialogues always touch the most profound levels of my existence.

Living organisms have been part of the symbiosis of nature over hundreds of millions of years. Human beings have been receiving the nurturing rhythm and flow of nature for thousands of years. Through astronomical changes, such as the movement and rotation of the sun, the moon and stars, as well as the cycle of seasonal changes, nature brings energy to our life. Moreover, as a member of the animal kingdom, human beings are the only species that has been given the ability of free will and self-reflection. Consequently, we are the only living beings on the Earth that are curious enough to discover our position within the unimaginable, infinite cosmos and its energy fields.

Caroline Myss is a renowned authority on contemporary spirituality and the science of energy medicine. She gives talks on energy medicine and western alchemy around the globe, stating that the world is undergoing a process of transformation from a materialistic civilisation towards an energetic civilisation. She has pointed out that the secret of influential masters of internal alchemy is to live in the present moment - that they use their body as an experimental laboratory of alchemy until they reach a level whereby they can control the energy field of their own bodies. Specifically, they are able to keep out the interferences of other energy fields in order to maintain a very stable state of stillness and tranquillity, which in turn will eventually become a strong enough light for time and space transformation.

A few years ago, I met Caroline at a talk she was giving at the Findhorn Foundation, an eco-community in Scotland. I discovered that she is a great admirer of the 14th century Spanish nun Saint Teresa of Avila, so much so that she says she has regular verbal and written communications with her. Saint Teresa of Avila saw the human soul as a crystal globe.

A long term interest of internal alchemists is how the crystal light of our soul is able to transform each and every single cell of our body and turn them into a crystal-like transparent high energy light. That in turn can change our entire body into a high energy field of light, leading to deep inner transformation and the ability to travel within time and space.

Some people have told me that the Qi Gong I have been teaching is very much like this Western internal alchemy. In these present times, the Earth is undergoing a dramatic de-magnetising transformation. Consequently, the meridian system of the Earth has entered what could be termed as an age of chaos. Practicing internal alchemy is one way we can shield ourselves during these times of change.

To my amazement, the rich literature of classical Chinese external and internal alchemy is still relatively unknown to the international alchemical research community. However, intuitively, they've sensed the power of alchemical light and consciousness within the practice of Qi Gong. I can feel this through the strong interest in the Qi Gong classes I teach. No wonder there is a Chinese saying that "the world is constantly rotating in a circle". I sense that a 'gold mining' journey to the East to discover and follow the Dao has only just begun.

# Introduction

As a Chinese medicine practitioner I have treated people using acupuncture for many years. I have never stopped finding new and better ways to alleviate human pain and suffering. The reason I chose to become an acupuncturist is very simple - it is because acupuncture needles can be conveniently carried anywhere and the practice of acupuncture can create wonders so long as the acupuncturist can maintain and apply a good level of Qi.

Herbal medicine on the other hand is far more complicated. Herbs can be highly affected by their source, quality and factors such as transportation, storage, shelf-life, etc. can all influence effectiveness.

However, reality is often not as simple as theoretical understanding. Some people are afraid of acupuncture and its needles and thus refuse to be treated. Others may have a condition that is not suited to acupuncture. Therefore, I started thinking maybe it would be even more convenient, and efficient, if I could cure people by a simple, even 'magic' touch?

From this perspective, I became very interested in the internal alchemy practice of Daoism and the secret practice of Tibetan Buddhist Yoga. I was fascinated by the literature available which talked a lot about time and space transformation, such as rejuvenating older people back to their youth, the magic of travelling freely between heaven and Earth as well as about how to become immortal. I wondered where these ancient alchemy practitioners went to after 'transforming into light'. For those who succeeded in becoming immortal in what kind of wondrous place did they end up?

I began to seriously practice Qi Gong by following a number of different masters. Gradually, I could feel and manage the spontaneous Qi inside my body and use it to cure my own bodily discomforts. The energy of Qi that goes through the meridian system revealed itself to me for the first time while in a deeply relaxed state of meditation; I could 'see' a strong purple light even when my eyes were completely closed. Later on, when I started to learn the classics of Chinese alchemy, I came across a saying that said the Daoist sage Lao Zi travelled from the east with purple light. I wondered "Is this the same purple light I was able to see during meditation?"

In order to learn and practice more Dao, I made a trip to Lao Shan Mountain in the north east Daoist mountain areas of China in search of masters. One afternoon during this trip I was on Yangkou beach at the foot of Lao Shan. I focused my eyes on the mountain and watched and watched with attentiveness. All of a sudden, I saw purple light embracing the entire mountain and an image of star constellations appeared inside the light.

The next day, when I visited the famous Hun Yuan rock, I found a star constellation carved in the rock which was exactly the same as I had seen inside that purple light the day before. The masters I met told me that Lao Zi had practiced Dao on the Hun Yuan rock. So, I then decided to also practice Qi Gong on the rock - as I did so, I felt as light as a bird.

But at that time I still didn't really understand what internal alchemy was. I had practiced for many years and with different masters but I had not experienced what is called 'baby light', a big light ball that revolves inside the lower abdomen.

A little while later I left China for the UK and to start with knew only a few people. Because of this I became quite disengaged from social activities. Instead I used my time to practice Qi Gong for up to eight hours per day. Through the cultivation of my practice I finally experienced foetus breathing. After this the effectiveness of my treatments on patients dramatically improved. It was almost as if I could cure each patient's disease by some kind of magic touch. I had never imagined that practicing medicine could come so naturally and be so delightful.

In 1998, I attended an international publisher's conference held in Cambridge. I was writing my first book *Listen to Your Body – The Wisdom of the Dao* at the time and hoped I might be able to develop relationships with some publishing houses. Among the speakers of the conference were influential people from magazines such as *Nature* and *New Science*.

While listening to their speeches, I found that I was able to see a kind of light and surrounding energies emanating from them in various forms and degrees. For example, there was a very senior publisher with a very pale face who went to the stage to give his talk. I wasn't able to see his face clearly and I fell into a deep sleep. On another occasion, I could see a speaker's head had a big light coming from it but, in contrast, the light from his body was very small and weak.

The last speaker of the day was the chief editor of a world renowned journal. All of sudden, the lights were turned on to the centre of the stage where he was about to deliver his speech. I felt completely awake and excited in anticipation of receiving his words of wisdom. I saw this handsome middle aged man in formal business attire come up to the stage and start his talk. He went on to say how busy and how hard it was these days to find time to properly evaluate papers and so on and so forth. As I watched him very attentively, his body radiated a white light shadow - however there was no light coming from his head. He looked like some of those ancient historical relics and sculptures that have lost their head! I took a deep breath to make myself more relaxed and looked again. However, the same vision persisted.

After his talk, I found some free copies of the journal he edited and picked one up to read on my journey home. The moment I started reading through the lines of text, I sensed a lack of Qi. It made me feel so tired that I had to close it. At this moment, an enlightened thought came to my mind: no matter how hard a person works, if he or she has no light from their head, the results will be futile. Their output carries little substance and their chances of success will be very small. Nevertheless, at this stage, I was still troubled by the question "what is internal alchemy actually like?"

At an international conference of scientists and medical doctors I met an influential biophysicist professor who had done extensive research into bio-electrons and bio-light. He told me that everybody emanates different degrees of light known as an 'aura'. That is to say, in physicists' terminology, each person emits electromagnetic waves of different frequencies all the time. There is a wide range of frequencies of electromagnetic waves in a human body that can vary anywhere from ultra-low frequency waves to long waves, medium waves, short waves, ultra-short waves, micro-waves, infrared, visible light, up to very high frequency waves such as ultra-violet light.

Normally, the electromagnetic waves from humans are very weak. For instance, the visible light of the human body will emit 100 photons per square metre per second, which is the equivalent of a candle light from 20kms away. Therefore, with a bright background, it's no wonder we can't see a human being's body light or 'aura'. Even in darkness, the sensitivity of our eyes is not sufficient to detect light of such tiny magnitude. Furthermore, our vision is limited within a very narrow range of light wave frequencies. Much of the expansive range of electromagnetic waves by both frequency and length (e.g., ultra-low frequency wave, long wave, medium wave, short wave, ultra-short wave, micro-wave, infrared, ultra-violet wave, x-ray and gamma ray) are beyond human visual perception. In other words, we are totally blind when it comes to the world of these electromagnetic waves. Even if some electromagnetic waves from the human body were quite strong, we would still not be able to see them.

The professor went on to tell me that due to the growing need for satellites, remote sensory and highly-sensitive electromagnetic sensory science and technology has developed very quickly in the past few decades. As a result, the application of this modern sensory technology to life sciences (i.e. to see the human body's aura), has now become entirely feasible. For thousands of years, the aura remained a mystical concept. To some, it is considered superstition or a religious illusion spread by the ignorance of our ancestors. Today, with the advance of science and technology, we are able to understand it as a simple physical phenomenon.

This professor is not only a scholar in physics, but also in biology and medicine. He has a very open-minded attitude toward phenomena that are not yet within the realm of today's modern sciences. In explaining why some people can see 'auras' - especially when in certain Qi Gong states - he explained: "Take the example of colour-blindness with which we are all very familiar. People who are colour-blind are unable to differentiate the full spectrum of colours within visible light which the majority of people normally can. This is because these individuals are weaker in their ability to differentiate electromagnetic wave frequencies. In other words, their range of receivable electromagnetic waves is even narrower than ordinary people."

"Because they are fewer in number we categorise them as being 'abnormal' in some way. However, viewed from an opposite perspective, you could describe a group of people who are able to differentiate not only the spectrum of colours within the visible light range but also those within the wider range of the electromagnetic spectrum."

"To give an example, there are some people able to see ultra-violet light just as bees are able to, or they may see infrared just as snakes can or even have the eyesight equivalent to that of an eagle. The world through the eyes of these types of people is quite different from ours, i.e. they receive far more information than we do. Because they are the minority however, they are viewed as 'abnormal'. Ordinary people might decide that these 'abnormal' people are simply bragging or making things up. It is further denigrated by the fact that they are only equipped with language and concepts that are limited to describing a world as seen only within the visible light range. When words and concepts used to describe a world that is unknown to the majority they are bound to be inaccurate or incomprehensible which will then often create disbelief and confusion amongst the greater public."

Fortunately, as the professor went on to say, human beings have learned to become more and more tolerant of interpersonal differences. More importantly, the modern knowledge of highly-sensitive electromagnetic sensory science and technology has become well established and is, for example, widely applied in spy satellites. Therefore, all that is required is to combine different technologies that are specialised in detecting different electromagnetic waves, and use them to measure the aura of human beings. The development of these technologies was initially motivated by human distrust and thus produced for warfare and defence. But they are also capable of bringing benefits and help us attain a greater understanding of ourselves.

The professor also raised another interesting point. He pointed out that electromagnetic waves are not that different from sound waves. They are all waves. We all know that music is created by organising a sequence of sound waves. By creating various unique sequences of organised sound waves, we are able to express our emotions, be it joy, sadness, anger or serenity. Likewise, electromagnetic waves can formulate music, i.e. from this perspective that which comprises the aura represents a subtle 'music' but it's a music that most people cannot hear. That is to say, technically, we can record the sequence of an aura (various frequencies and lengths of electromagnetic waves) sent out by the human body within a period of time. In this way, we can obtain a record of a person's physiological, psychological and clinical dynamics in the same way as we can record a piece of music.

As detailed in the *Yellow Emperor's Classic of Internal Medicine*, the ancient Chinese paid a great deal of attention to the harmony between mind and body, as well as the oneness of Heaven and Man. The German composer Johann Sebastian Bach (1685-1750) also said the harmony of music comes from heaven; while off-harmony music is from hell. Interestingly, in English, the same word 'harmony' is used to describe both a pleasant, coordinated piece of music as well as a state of existence.

The Chinese Buddhist master Bai Yin said that the difference between heaven and hell is all in the mind. Said another way, both heaven and hell are inside our mind. We can either instantly go up to heaven or down to hell. In fact, even without being experts in music, we can all recognise that music is closely related to psychological and physiological conditions. Also, one need not have much knowledge of music in order to differentiate the music of heaven from the music of hell.

Just as we can gauge, record and analyse music that is formed by sound waves, we can also do the same with the 'music' formed by electromagnetic waves and we can therefore objectively record the sequence of the human aura's electromagnetic waves, and quantitatively analyse the 'music' produced by the stream of these waves. This recording will reveal objectively the state of body and mind, judging easily if the person is in sync with heaven or with hell.

In Western medicine, there is a new line of research and practice which has blossomed recently, called 'psychosomatic medicine'. It investigates the relationships between psychological states and diseases, including cancer, high blood pressure and diabetes etc. Common sense dictates that if a person is consistently living in sync with hell, he or she will evidently become sick sooner or later. On the contrary, if a person is often living in sync with heaven, he or she will be quite healthy.

From the professor's point of view, the practice of internal alchemy is all about reforming and improving one's state of mind. Or to put it another way, it is to practice and fine-tune our internal music. When you are able to fill your heart with harmonious music from the heavens all the time, you will be healthy and live a long life. When everybody's hearts are filled with harmonious music from the heavens, guess what happens? The whole world will be as happy and harmonious as the heavens.

**This is how modern physics has opened the door towards the understanding of internal alchemy for me.**

In ancient times, internal alchemy was a practice whereby practitioners used their own bodies like a laboratory to study and experiment with immortality. One of the milestones of this journey was to cultivate a 'child of light' so that one could develop a new found sense of freedom. In doing so they were then capable of extra-sensory perception which aided the development of more functions than the human body seemed capable. This included developing the cultivation of Jing-Qi-Shen (Essence-Energy-Spirit) and The Qi's of the Five Elements (fire – heart; wood – liver; metal – lung; earth – stomach; water –

kidney). The alchemic blending of these elements allowed practitioners to access higher cosmic dimensions and in so doing they could then change bodily forms, multi-locate and astral-travel. At this last stage, one's spirit can travel through space and time or migrate to the lands of the immortals (to planets lived in by higher, more advanced civilisations). Therefore, the goal of internal alchemy was to achieve something called "The merging of heaven and human as one" and "heaven and human work/create as one".

**The purpose of this book is to explain ancient internal alchemy so that it can be understood today.**

China has contributed to the understanding of internal alchemy in a very significant way. It has accumulated a long history with substantial literature and contributions from numerous schools of practice. Daoism alone has yielded some 8,000 to 10,000 books relating to the theory and techniques of alchemy. This literature records that many people had reached high levels of internal alchemy, for example records showed that before the Song dynasty, there were already tens of thousands of people whom had reached a level of ability that allowed them to 'space-travel'.

Many ancient poems and essays, as well as many important Chinese classical novels, such as *Journey to the West*, *Dreams of the Red Chamber*, *Stories of Immortals*, have in one way or another, touched upon aspects of internal alchemy, be it the processes of, or the consequent results. In addition to Lao Zi who was highly specialised in internal alchemy, other well-known alchemists included Wei Bo Yang, Zhang Zhong Jing, Ge Hong, Sun Si Miao, Tao Hong Jing and Li Shi Zheng. The greatest poets Li Bai and Su Shi were also practitioners and advocates of internal alchemy.

The 'essence, Qi and spirit' of internal alchemy, as well as the meridian system became the founding building blocks of Chinese internal medicine, and together with the *Book of Changes* created the Eastern philosophy of 'the Heaven, Earth, Human trinity and oneness'. It gave rise to a civilisation that aspired to harmonious co-existence between man and heaven (cosmos, other planets), man and Earth (Feng Shui, environmental geology) and man and man (society).

External alchemy practices and their experiments became the forerunners of modern chemistry and lent its technologies to the early smelting industry leading to the production of bronze, gunpowder and the invention of the compass, to name just a few. The wealth generated by the material and technological advancement allowed the $14^{th}$ century mariner Zheng He to build a fleet of ships that launched his voyages to introduce the high civilisation of the Middle Kingdom, namely China, to the rest of the world.

It is not an exaggeration to say that alchemy created the Chinese civilisation. This ancient civilisation has the capacity to continue with this tradition for the benefit of the entirety of human civilisation, leading human beings to evolve into a new phase in their evolution.

'To lead mankind' should not be a mere slogan, but a disciplined practice of 'heaven and human as one'. The Heaven refers to the cosmos and to the spirit (Shen). Only human beings who have hearts that have become as bright as gold can then merge with heaven. This unity of heaven and human will then facilitate their movements to flow in accordance with Dao, consolidating Earth's energy and Qi field. They will train others and allow more human beings to reach the golden heart standard and help them to gradually and smoothly walk toward a new existence and a new era.

This higher level of consciousness is characterised by compassion and action towards the harmony of the entire cosmos.

We have arrived at a juncture in time where immortals and mortals will live and work together. What does that mean? It means that some human beings will evolve into being immortal. That is human beings and immortals becoming as one. The immortal is a representation of the wisdom and consciousness of the cosmos. It also means that higher civilisations in the cosmos will come to Earth to participate and facilitate in the evolution of the Earth. The wisdom of immortals will use vehicles, such as Chinese medicine, internal alchemy practices and theories of harmony and creativity to elevate the human soul and consciousness. The elevated human consciousness in turn will exert energy and light to carry on the actions of Dao which is to protect the Dao of the Earth.

This will uphold the concepts of 'Immortals hold up the Dao of the world' and 'Internal alchemy works towards Dao'.

**This can all begin from self-improvement, i.e. to love one another, to love oneself, and to purify oneself.** In time, immortals and mortals will work and live together to create a harmonious society, world and cosmos.

# Part One

# Chapter One
## Internal Alchemy for Immortality

Throughout history, and all over the world, there have always been people who choose to completely devote their lives to the practice of, and experimentation with, internal alchemy.

What is it that makes internal alchemy so attractive to these individuals? In Chinese, alchemy means 'the technique of smelting Dan'. Therefore Dan is the product and desired result of the entire process of smelting (practices). What then is 'Dan'? Dan means a high frequency light and energy field. The 'techniques of smelting Dan' is the ability to tune into frequencies and have access to the frequencies throughout the entire range of the electromagnetic spectrum. From time to time we hear about some people who are able to perform miracles - for instance, a traditional doctor who is able to see a patient's internal organs or the stones inside the kidney or gallbladder. This kind of special ability, along with seeing things with x-ray vision, hearing sounds from supernaturally long distances, sensing or foreseeing earthquakes, and so on, are all instances of people who are able to tune in and/or have access to frequencies that normal human beings do not.

When a person has achieved the process of internal alchemy or, in other words, obtained Dan through smelting, he or she will be able to tune into any kind of frequency wherever and whenever he or she wishes. That ability is referred to as "the connection to the cosmos, to the self, and to others" - in other words the total awakening or enlightenment of our consciousness. One can say that the essence of internal alchemy is to realise the hidden potentials of the human being. The process of this self-realisation is characterised by discovering one's internal light. At the end of this self-realisation, one will have fully comprehended what constitutes the human body and the whole cosmos, what the meaning of life is, what human beings' place in the universe is, where we have come from, and where we are going to. In short, internal alchemy is the practice which leads to the ultimate liberation, freedom and harmony which man has always craved.

The so-called 'smelting Dan' technique is the method of practice which purifies the energy field of the human body; to purify the human body from dimness, darkness and mixed colours into pure gold or pure white, or golden and white light. It is like smelting the heavy metal of iron and turning it into gold.

When the body has turned into pure golden or white light, the body creates a very strong field with high energy and high frequency and a wide range of frequency vibration. The heat of white and golden light will be able to dissolve any disease. People with such a pure and high energy field have not only completely liberated themselves, but are also able to help other people to resolve their problems and enlighten others' paths to immortality.

The ancient classics said, "Once you have achieved 'Dan', you will not die in the water or fire". This may simply sound like a piece of fictitious human mythology. However, imagine if your field of Qi has turned into golden or white light, you will be like gold and silver that can be ruined by neither water, nor fire. You will be as impervious as a diamond.

Modern physics has discovered that when three quarks form in a pyramid structure, the structure turns to white and transforms into an empty state of transparent white light. When a person is able to enter into this state of emptiness that is when creation starts (like in the cell process known as mitosis). In that state of transparent white light and emptiness a person will be able to multi-locate, like in the story of *The Seven Daoist Masters* where Daoist master Wang Chong Yang was able to teach Sun Bu Er in a separate room whilst still engaging with others elsewhere.

A state of emptiness is very important in elevating the energy field. Many spiritual practices emphasise the emptiness of the mind. Many methods such as silence and meditation are aimed at entering a state of emptiness. Emptiness is not numbness and is not a withdrawal from reality. It is a prerequisite to becoming enlightened. It is to be empty of impurity in order to be filled with pure light. It is a necessary step in the processes involved in upgrading the energy levels. Only by reaching a state of serenity, are you then able to return to the root of humanity and the genesis of the world.

The practice of the soul and spirituality is to become enlightened by an awakening to your own inner light. This is opposite to becoming attached to an external God, which often turns into a worldly power or can lead to global power struggles and wars.

Regardless of what methods of practice you follow, they all lead to the same place. It is a state of completeness and/or a state of pure and high energy capable of tuning into a wider range of frequencies.

Throughout history this can be seen in many alchemical practices such as:
- The phenomenon of the 'rainbow body (虹化)' of some Tibetan Buddhist traditions.
- The eight Daoist immortals crossing the sea, in which these individuals travelled through space and time.
- In the West, a bishop who practiced internal alchemy whereby his body did not decompose even after 900 years.

- A Western priest, Padre Peo who was recorded as being able to multi-locate.
- Jesus, it is claimed, was a practitioner of the ancient Eastern mystical practices, and this enabled him to perform various miracles, such as stopping a woman's bleeding by a simple touch.
- In the Jiu Hua (九华) Mountains of China, there are several Buddhist monks' bodies that have lasted as long as a thousand years.
- In Chinese history, there was a famous doctor, Zhang Zhong Jing (张仲景), who cured many people during widespread and serious contagious epidemics without himself being affected.

All these legends are telling us one thing - internal alchemy is a pathway towards immortality and, as such, is beyond material existence.

Ancient Daoist schools believe that the human body itself is a micro-cosmos which is strongly connected to the macro-cosmos. Other planets and galaxies also host countless civilisations. Our ancestors understood this. In the classics, they kept telling us that "there will always be mountains beyond the mountains, and there will always be universes outside of the universe".

The higher civilisations that exist in the cosmos can select and communicate with human beings who possess high energy fields judging from the degree of purity and brightness of their aura. The analogy of this concept within modern times is the transistor radio. This type of communication technology allows us to connect with one another but only if we can tune into the same frequency through these devices.

The heavens that we wish to go to after our death are images of higher civilisations on other planets or dimensions that exist in higher energy fields. Images of these can come to us when we have entered a very relaxed and deep state of stillness. The reason we can then see them is because our energy fields become tuned into the same frequencies of the energy fields of these higher civilisations. That is how we become connected - we effectively experience space travel at the speed of light within a high energy vibration field.

It sounds unbelievable to most people. However, this is common knowledge among those who have reached a certain energetic level - they were called 'true beings' (真人) and 'realised beings' (至人) in ancient times. In the *Yellow Emperor's Classics of Internal Medicine*, the yellow emperor said: "in higher antiquity there were 'true beings' and in middle antiquity, there were 'realised beings', who had pure virtue and attained complete understanding, could tune into nature, had accumulated sufficient levels of living essence and spirit, could travel freely between heaven and Earth and saw and heard things from very remote places..."

The 'true being' and 'realised being' are beings that can remain in that high frequency field, whereas some more ordinary people may only occasionally, or even accidentally, enter this field. Such an experience of 'space travel' can often be referred to as breathtaking and as only a 'once in a lifetime' event as they will then drop back into their ordinary low frequency field, i.e. into the world we have come to believe as being the only reality. This momentary experience of the truth of the universe can appear to be an illusory dream, or indeed nothing more than our wild imagination. Some might use it as a source of literary creativity that can inspire science fiction stories as well as creating other forms of artistic expression. However some people might end up in doctors and psychiatrists' clinics only to then be diagnosed as being psychotic.

People who have either practiced substantial internal alchemy or who have had profound Buddhist meditation experiences often acquire special abilities. For example, when they look very attentively at a person, they may be able to see the aura on top of that person's head and the body can be seen as an X-ray image, i.e. the body becomes half transparent or an image that is filled with faint light shadows. When looking at a group of people from a distance, they will see various shapes of light shadow images. Some could be in red light; others in yellow light; or half bright, half dim; or light legs but dark higher up; or light on the head but dark below. Some can however be perceived to be in skeletal form only. I have also known people who are able to tell the colour and quality of aura of their friends and relatives living overseas. Some people have seen images or heard music and sounds that can't be found anywhere on Earth. Such phenomena are termed as being 'special faculties'. However, these faculties are not really special at all, as all human beings innately have them as a birthright.

Let us consider the electromagnetic spectrum which we may have learnt at school. On this spectrum, only a very narrow range of waves are visible to our human eyes whereas the rest of the spectrum we are unable and have no idea how to 'see'. However, the so-called 'special faculties' are abilities that can be accessed through rigorous training and practice that allow people to see or hear (perceive) beyond the normal visible range. People with 'special faculties' develop them to such an extent that they can adjust their bodies' vibrational frequency to the same spectrum as, for example, X-ray or ultra-violet waves. With regards to special hearing faculties, they are able to perform just like a radio does in that they can set their frequency to the middle, long or short band wave frequency. These abilities, in ancient practice, were known as the 'six miracle connections'.

People with 'special faculties' could tune into, say, infrared and ultra-violet wave frequencies to treat diseases such as infections and inflammation. Some of them use a focused consciousness to 'see' the swollen area, others use relaxed stillness to 'think' about the patient's inflammation - in either case the inflammation will in all likelihood disappear. They are applying light and sound waves just like gamma rays or laser beams. We sometimes come across these kinds of situations in our ordinary lives and we ourselves are capable at differing degrees of such feats. Once I was told by a teacher who taught at the Beijing Chinese Medicine College that during the peak of Qi Gong's popularity in China, the president of the college received a research grant and conducted research that produced fascinating results. One paper published showed that a Qi Gong master's brain waves in a state of stillness had become Taiji (太极) shaped. Another interesting paper, which was not published, described how some Qi Gong masters were able to produce Qi that contained infrasound waves. Science has shown that infrasound waves can go around the Earth several times without dissipating. Some countries have researched infrasound waves to develop weapons. But they can also become a 'weapon' to cure cancer. It is a double-edged sword - no wonder that in ancient practice, one always practiced virtue first before practicing and developing 'special faculties.' Using very powerful electronic telescopes, modern scientists have observed that some galaxies are rotating or interacting based on a Taiji pattern which only confirms that our bodies are a micro-cosmos that epitomise the macro-cosmos in essence. This is the holographic view of "heaven and human as one".


When I read Stephen Hawking's book, *"A Brief History of Time"*, I was thrilled to learn that although the colour of quarks can be arranged into 36 types, when three basic quarks form together the entity becomes white. Moreover, when we combine all electromagnetic waves, the resultant colour is also white. That is the state of 'complete oneness' (大圆满). This reminds me of a particular anecdote. One day, I recalled that some patients of mine, after treatment, had not come back to visit me. I wondered if this meant that they got better or perhaps had stopped coming because my treatment had not been effective? The very next day one of these patients came to my clinic – it was as if he had read my mind and heard my query. He told me "I've come to see you not because I have any discomfort. I made this appointment just to let you know what happened after you last treated me." His story goes as follows:

"Seven years ago I came to your clinic for my knee pain problem and you treated me with acupuncture. I only came for three treatments and after the third treatment, I felt very relaxed. On my way back home, someone caught my attention from behind and asked me where I was going. This person turned out to be an old friend of mine. I told him that I was just on my way back from an acupuncture treatment and that I felt great. This friend then said: 'You are surrounded by a white light ball. The white light is very bright and it radiates too.' I thought to myself, 'I must stay in this white light, it feels great. I feel not only no pain, but also very light and carefree.' I also remembered what you had told me that no matter what I do, I need not be anxious about it. I need to give myself more space, avoid rushing myself with tight scheduling which will inevitably end up causing anxiety. I really followed your advice and reminded myself from time to time to 'stay in the white light, don't go out of it, and don't get anxious.' Since then, my leg and knee have never had any problem and I haven't suffered from any other health problem either."

This patient had developed an enlightened consciousness. His anecdote reminds me of a story in the Chinese classic *The Journey to the West*, where at one point, Sun Wu Kong (孙悟空) the monkey, used his golden stick to draw a circle and asked the rest of the team travelling with him to stay inside this circle for protection. The monk named Sha, followed this advice and stayed inside the circle. As a result, he was safely protected. However in the case of the pig, seduced by beautiful women and delicious food, he left the circle and ended up being captured by a demon masquerading to be a beautiful woman. Monk Sha understood an important principle of internal alchemy, which is the principle of 'staying centred' (守中). By being able to 'stay centred' it allows you to stay under the protection of a high energy field. It requires that one does not become a slave to one's own desire for sensual gratification. The pig, on the other hand, was led by his greed, sexual desire, possessiveness and so on, all of which are characterised by very low and heavy energy fields. It is the demon's field. As a result, the pig was only enchanted by appearances and was unable to see the truth of the evil motives of who was in front of him and, consequently, was eventually captured by the demon. The conflict, struggle and warfare among human beings are results of the same low and heavy energy fields. It is a state called 'being infatuated by demons'.

A Chinese medicine doctor says: "When the positive Qi is kept inside, the bad Qi will be futile". When the pig violated the principle of internal alchemy, his Qi was no longer inside, but rather was leaking out. Therefore, the demons could go inside and attack him. Once you are under the influence of a demon, you will naturally feel helpless and fatigued. It is a very common phenomenon that when you are controlled by external forces, you are likely to exaggerate the power of these forces, hence become more frightened by them. Fear hurts the kidneys which are the source of living energy and creativity (according to Chinese medicine theory); that in turn will lead to a defensive mode of thinking and behaviour, which will further escalate conflict. When you enter this vicious cycle, an enormous amount of poison will be generated which can seriously harm the body and cause various diseases, namely hopelessness, depression, anxiety, pain and psychotic or neurotic problems.

On Earth, the human body's energy or vibration field has changed a lot. It is directly influenced by our diet, our mental state and our lifestyle. At the same time, we are affected by the magnetic field of the Earth, as well as other planets in every moment. If we do not make a conscious effort to practice and cultivate ourselves, our energy vibration will decrease. We will feel heavier and heavier to a point that any feelings of heavenly lightness will become totally foreign to us.

When talking about internal and external alchemy, people in China associate this with Tai Shang Lao Ju (太上老君) which, in Chinese legend, is Lao Zi's immortal image up in heaven in a smelting furnace of Dan, or, instead, mysterious Daoists surrounded in mists of Dan smoke.

These figures and images can be found in temples or caves wearing Daoist robes and engaged in some sort of religious ritual. People generally treat these images as mythology and therefore totally irrelevant to their existing reality. As for Qi Gong practitioners, they think it is very difficult or even impossible to obtain the secret Dan scripture (or in western terminology, the Akashic Records) – that there is no way to learn it, unless a white bearded immortal in the depths of the mountains agrees to teach it to you.

**Tai Shang Lao Ju (太上老君)**

Nobody imagines that this immortal golden Dan actually radiates from within and is available in every moment of our ordinary daily lives.

China has a long and unique history of internal alchemy. There are many schools of alchemy practitioners that have developed different methods of training and practice. Records show that before the Song Dynasty, there were a hundred thousand people who reached the level of 'Chong Ju'. 'Chong Ju' means that after training and practicing, one has accumulated a 'high energy ball of light' inside of one's abdomen. Inside this ball of light lies an inner child containing all information and images of the person. This golden ball of light goes up from one's abdomen along the central meridian all the way to the top of one's head and comes out of the head to then connect with the universe and makes possible the ability to 'space travel.' With such a description, a person would probably conjure up an image of a space shuttle launching.

People interested in internal alchemy may have heard the terms 'dissolved corpse' (尸解) and 'flying to the heavens' (白日昇飛) both of which mean astral travel. These and others are descriptions of the transformation of spiritual energy. Spiritual energy is like a driver and the body is merely a vehicle. If you do not take care of your vehicle, it will break down. Therefore the driver will have to change vehicles. That is why we say the training of internal alchemy will lead us to have the ability to transcend both life and death.

The biggest contribution, as well as the most unique characteristic of Chinese internal alchemy, is its comprehensive understanding of the human meridian system. This comprehensive understanding came from thousands of people's own internal experiments, as well as rigorous training and self-exploration. This is the biggest contribution that Chinese internal alchemy has made to the entire human race. Nowhere else on Earth had such a system been developed with such a thorough and accurate record and understanding of the invisible truths contained within the human body.

To be more specific, meridian theory has the following important areas to contribute:
1. The pathway and precondition whereby heaven, Earth and human being can merge into oneness and the method whereby a person can consciously experience both their body energy and spiritual energy to the point where they

come into resonance and mutually recognise each other.
2. The experimentation and proof of how high energy light can be generated as a result of practice.
3. An index for diagnosis and treatment of disease and understanding of the regulation of light distribution within meridians in terms of how it is related to the pathology of disease.

For instance, when a person has light throughout the body but with no light in the area of the head, he or she will appear to have a weak mind and lack creativity. They may work very hard, but their activities often don't lead anywhere. The opposite will be individuals who have big light around head but a dim light surrounding the body. In this case, people use their brain too much and their body's meridians are blocked and therefore they become physically unhealthy.

Over twenty years ago, I held a Qi Gong retreat in the mountains of Wales. Before the class, I arrived and stayed with one of my students who lived nearby the retreat venue. Her husband had a brother who also lived in the same building and asked to meet with me to have a chat. My student's brother-in-law was, at the time, following a female yoga master and very faithfully practicing Indian yoga. We met and, whilst chatting with him, I sensed his whole body to be very cold, his face very pale, and that he was very hungry. I asked him what practices he engaged in. He said his practice included meditation and fasting (not eating or eating less). He claimed that his master's Qi field was very powerful and even took me to see this master's picture hanging on a wall in his bedroom. When I saw this picture, I could sense the weakness of her body and it was quite damaged. I asked about her health condition and I was not surprised at all to find out that she had abdominal cancer. Even though she had developed a large light that surrounded her head, her lower body meridians were all blocked. She was suffering from a very serious health condition.

**A combination of spiritual practice and physical body practice is the way toward the enlightening of the whole self.**

Physical movement and guiding Qi to flow easily throughout the meridian system are both Earth and human practices, whereas practicing the virtue of mind and soul leads to a cultivation of light within the heart and head - this is a heaven practice. In the classic books of Chinese internal alchemy, we often read the following phrase: "The heavenly practice leads to the big Dan, the Earthly practice leads to immortal Dan and the humanly practice leads to golden Dan". Therefore, each kind of practice is equally important. One must open up his or her entire body's meridian system, which cannot be simply achieved through reading classics or practicing meditation and stillness. To conduct heavenly practice, one has to cultivate selflessness and speak and act according to one's conscience during everyday life. When you live with these principles, you will have no fear in life and you will always be supported by heaven.

# Chapter Two
# 'Heaven, Earth and Human as One' – The Password of our Civilisation

'Heaven, Earth and Human as One' is the new code for raising the consciousness of human beings and renewing the Earth. Before our human civilisation appeared, there had been quite advanced civilisations that had existed here. However, they conducted experiments that misused the environment and water causing a deadly environmental collapse which consequently made the Earth totally uninhabitable. In other words, their action and behaviour led them to a tragedy of total self-destruction.

When, the creation of a new civilisation began, wise men learned to focus on harmony between nature and human beings. Information, more importantly the natural laws and orders contained in the *Yi Jing* (易经) *Book of Changes*, was introduced by advanced souls who had been reincarnated in human form to reveal the wisdoms of the cosmos. This wisdom spoke of how human beings needed to respect nature and follow the rules of the natural environment - by learning the core teachings of Feng Shui and to refrain from being disrespectful or excessively playful with the Earth.

The wise men or sages from different human civilisations had all received this message to some extent. The Mayan calendar also has the eight trigrams within it, as well as the image of the Taiji symbol which both depict the spiralling galaxies and cosmos. The pyramids of Egypt were constructed to draw the heavenly energy's power down to the Earth. In the West, an organisation called the Freemasons was devoted to the task of rebuilding the meridians of the Earth. For hundreds of years they were secretly engaged in the planning and building of churches on the right locations in order to balance the Qi field of the Earth. The needle shaped church towers acted like acupuncture needles on the body of the Earth. It was no accident that churches were designed to have needle shaped towers pointing to the heavens as well as large, round dome halls to host human worship activities.

One time while in discussion with the biophysicist professor I wrote about in the introduction, I asked him why the three important human Dantian (energy centres) all resided in the centre of the three anatomical body cavities? He replied that it made huge sense as the centre of a cavity is the focal point of all waves - hence it contains the highest field of energy. He mentioned an old tradition in Europe whereby, before a big battle, soldiers would go to a church and pray under the centre of the hall's dome as this would make them feel calm. This tradition tells of the strong energy focusing effect of the centre of a round shaped structure. This reasoning is also behind our practices of the body's Dantian which are focal points to accumulate Qi and light.

On several occasions many years ago now, I was invited to attend a number of 'Freemason Ladies' Parties'. This kind of party is held to express gratitude to the mothers and wives who had been providing continuous support to the Freemasons' hard work. The organisation of the Freemasons itself is formed exclusively of male members. They are able to channel information from the higher spirit realms, and carry out worldly affairs according to the guidance of the heavenly messages they receive. One of their important projects was to build churches to ensure the Earth held a good quality Qi field. They have a thorough process of screening and selecting new members. George Washington, one of the founding fathers of the United States of America, and the musical genius Mozart were known members. Because the organisation conducts their projects in a very low key way and in a rather secretive manner, some people view it as a clandestine cult.

However, to my surprise, I met at these ladies' parties many existing friends who turned out to be Freemasons. At these parties, they read out poems and sang songs to celebrate their beloved women. They were very joyful and harmonious. A mayor and a chief of the police were among them. The last item on any party's agenda is always a fund raising activity for a charity. They say that donating money to public welfare is one of their practice methods for attaining enlightenment.

**To build human constructions in a manner that correspond with astronomical alignments is a way to unite the energy of the heaven, the earth and human beings. It can generate huge energy that helps create advanced cultures and civilisations.**

Xian and Beijing in China were built according to the 'River Diagram' (河图) and the 'Luo Writing' (洛书), two diagrams said to have been channelled from heaven. The Forbidden City in Beijing was, as mentioned earlier, built in accordance with the Ursa Minor/Zi Wei star constellation, whereas the city of Nanjing was built in accordance to the Tian Shi star constellation. The societies created by these centres had led China to become very advanced among the world's civilisations around the time of the 13th century.

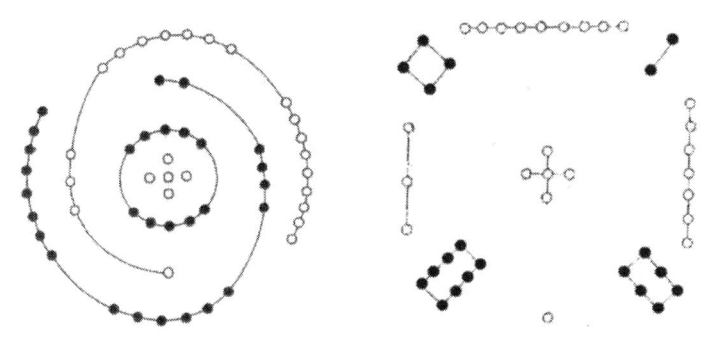

**River Diagram 河图 and the Luo Writing 洛书**

Planners in England and France tried to do the same with their cities. However, because existing residents refused to co-operate, it was impossible to build the individual cities completely in accordance to astronomical orders. The planners could only partially achieve what they had set out to do. Therefore, England and France did not reach their full potential on the world stage. When the United States was established, the capital of the nation, Washington DC, was built from scratch. They built it based on astronomical orders. Each government building that was constructed corresponded with an astronomical sign and made up the twelve constellations of the Western Zodiac. Consequently, the US then went on to become a world leader and has remained powerful for many years.

Aside from civil engineering endeavours and society building with the aim of realising heaven and human correspondence, Daoists received many heavenly messages to achieve the same purpose from an inward perspective. They were taught to respect nature, to observe nature and to understand nature, so that man would not interfere and harm nature. They were also taught to use their own body to be the practicing and experimental ground for developing advanced abilities that included accessing energetic information systems, for fine-tuning energy vibration levels and the exercising of self-purification practices.

During Daoist training and practice, one should always appreciate what is offered by nature, and learn from nature. For instance, we can learn from the sun and the moon - both of which radiate light - that each give us energy and simply exist without asking for anything in return. It is a completely selfless and unconditional giving which never stops, even when they are not asked to do so. The sun and the moon shine in accordance with the Dao, as well as indicating what is needed to live our lives. Daoist appreciation is so sincere and deep that no words can adequately capture it. Therefore, Daoists seek to express their deep gratitude by actions within their practice of daily living.

Many Qi Gong training methods were developed based on ancient Daoist beliefs and wisdoms of worshipping nature. Daoists like to live in the mountains as they are natural pyramids that connect heaven and Earth. They absorb the Qi of the five elements - metal, wood, water, fire and earth - within the mountain as well as eat wild fruits, herbs and water from the mountain springs. In so doing, they cultivate their five internal organs to be in harmony with the five elements. They walk in the pattern of the Ba Gua Zhen (The Eight Diagrams of Daoist Cosmology) stepping sequence and, in the evening, they follow the patterns of the stars and constellations of the night sky in order to experiment between the relationships of the body's internal organs and astronomical patterns.

An Australian friend of mine, a certified Chinese medicine doctor, has an immune system disease. To treat his problem, he started to practice Ba Gua martial arts and walk the Ba Gua stepping sequence that was taught to him. He is now over sixty years old but walks like a flying bird.

In my Qi Gong classes, I arrange practices based on the laws of Yin and Yang in accordance with the sun and the moon in order to receive the energy coming from the cosmos. When the sun rises, one should correspond to Yang but practice the Yin and nourish the liver; when the sun sets, one should correspond to Yin but practice Yang and nourish the lung and kidney; at noon one should be quiet to help the Yin to nourish the heart; and lastly at midnight one should meditate and calm down the Yin to give rise to Yang. People who follow the daily rhythm of these practices never catch any colds or have other health problems. Through these practices, they are developing the abilities to be able to connect with the high energy field of the cosmos.

The primary aim of internal alchemy - or the smelting of Dan - is to purify the Qi field, to smelt the energy field of the human body and mind that contains lots of impurities and turn this into pure essence – as embodied by immortals. This pure essence is a high vibration field characterised by golden and white lights. When human beings evolve to this level, they will naturally do things that will only benefit the Earth and fellow humans.

These advanced individuals can vibrate in union with the high frequencies of the cosmos. Their sensual feelings will naturally differ from ordinary people. They are very sensitive and able to feel, see and hear remotely, i.e. conduct communication at distance without the need for a telephone or computer. They do not need to rely on the material world much to sustain their existence. For instance, they can adjust their body temperature to endure various weather conditions and therefore can live comfortably without heating and air conditioning equipment. Also, the ways they intake energy completely changes whereby they can obtain nature's energy through digesting light and Qi through their meridian system and skin. This, therefore, allows them to live with very little or no food. Thus, the need to take animals' lives and turning wild vegetation into farm land becomes unnecessary. If enough humans reached this higher state of being, the 'need' to exploit other people, animals and the natural world for survival would become history. At such a time, the Earth would become a most exquisite field of gardens.

In a Qi Gong class offered by a Chinese Medicine Department at an English University, I met a student who was quite weak physically. He loved nature and from early childhood onwards he had watched almost all natural history TV programmes that had been broadcast. He said he felt most drawn towards Daoism because Daoism was about the oneness of heaven, earth and humans.

At the age of 19, he began to learn Taiji from a Taiji master. When he was in my Qi Gong class, I found that he, more often than not, liked to spend time alone and meditate. He was very critical towards the youth drug culture and the 'hanging out in bars' type of lifestyle that so many others his age adopted. In the evening, his friends and classmates all went to bars to have a drink, but he chose not to go. He would rather practice meditation either in sitting or lying down postures. He said that when he was 14 years old, he started to practice meditation according to a book called the "treatise on sitting and forgetting." After that, he found that he became very indifferent toward his parents' emotional dramas. He became scared of entering into a state of emotional detachment, so he stopped any further practice.

When he was in my class, he always asked me to tell him more internal alchemy theory. I taught him the method of practice that I described earlier, i.e. to practice at sunrise, midday, sunset and midnight (otherwise known as Zi-Wu-Mao-You Practice). However, he did not continue with this practice. After I moved on, he started to follow a Taiji teacher again to continue building up his physical strength. He spent more time practicing moving Qi to the tendons, bones, and skin using mind-directed consciousness. At the same time, he continued to practice meditation in sitting and lying down postures on an irregular basis. After a while, his body became much stronger. Some fellow classmates could see that his body had a white light around it. His lower Dantian was full which made him feel great. At the age of 24 when he began to teach Qi Gong, his disposition came across as wanting to be heroic. At this time he began to date a girl who had very weak Qi. After only three months of dating, the white light he had once harboured was gone. He declared that he was no longer interested in Daoism. He stopped his vegetarian diet and began eating meat.

I have seen several cases like this throughout my teaching career. These individuals treat Qi Gong as a way to build up their body's physical strength but they are not fully committed. Therefore, they cannot consistently keep connecting their personal energy field with the larger energy field of heaven and Earth. As such, they are not able to establish a stable Qi field. Moreover, they lack spirit or desire to be connected with the energies of higher spiritual realms. They are likely to be indulgent to physical sensations and become slaves to sensual gratification. As a result, the fire of Dan will extinguish within them. It is not unlike the case where materials that have the potential to turn into gold end up being scrap iron through not being cultivated properly.

For humans, eating meat is one of the reasons why the frequency of our Qi remains in the third dimension. We still have many characteristics of wild animals. We can be selfish, attached to sensual pleasure, and can easily enter into fierce wars and competitions for survival, and so on. These are all manifestations of low energy fields. It prevents us from hearing and receiving messages from the higher cosmos. As a result, while the *Yi Jing* brought us the truth of the universe, we now think of it as myth.

There are many practices that have existed for thousands of years that help decode the secret password of 'heaven, earth and human as one'. In the West, there were practices of small and big mysticism. In the East, there was the Tantric path of Tibetan Buddhism and Daoist internal alchemy. All of these practices are passed on secretly - the higher the level, the more secretive they are. By keeping the secret, silence, and meditation, one will be able to accumulate Qi and light, which in turn will enable the practitioner to elevate their energy field and enter into the state of 'heaven, earth and human as one'.

When you fully open your meridian points and begin to feel how the changes of the cosmos and the Earth interact with your body, your energy changes and you begin to experience the vibration or movement of your body in alignment with the vibrations of the cosmos and the Earth. This is what's called spontaneous Qi Gong. In Qi Gong classes, occurrences of spontaneous Qi Gong can be very common. Usually, the Qi will go to the origins of health problems that will then lead to self-healing.

When maintaining high level Qi Gong practices, the human body's Qi will flow in accordance with the rhythm of the Earth's movement and form a daily cycle. For example, when the Yang rises and the Yin sets, bodily Qi and fluids will exchange accordingly. The Qi in the organs will flow according to the Chinese twelve hour cycle of two hour periods. For example, noon is associated with the heart Qi whereby the Yin fluids drop down through until 5-7pm, the period associated with the lungs. Then the lung Qi nourishes the kidney Qi which is birthed between 11pm-1am which in turn nourishes the liver Qi at sunrise. The heart Qi arises once more and the cycle begins again. For more details on this daily cycle, please refer to my earlier book *Listen To Your Body*.

Furthermore, the human body also changes in accordance with the monthly moon's orbit of the Earth and this is called the 'small heavenly cycle'. One time, in a Qi Gong retreat in England, we practiced how to obtain Qi from a full moon and use it to cultivate the five elements to open up the major meridians of the body. The best practice time tends to be about 10:30pm when the full moon rises up in a clear sky. At this time, our whole class went outside and we practiced for about two hours. After practicing, Sarah a retired school teacher who was very sensitive, came to me and asked, "Did I do something wrong? I felt that the Qi rose from the left side of my body and fell down on the right, rather than rising from the back spine (Du meridian) and going down the front (Ren meridian). Why is that so?"

I found a perfect opportunity to teach a little more about Qi Gong through their firsthand experiences. In addition to the rise and fall cycle of the Du and Ren meridians, there is another cycle that exists on either side of the navel where liver Qi rises on the left and lung Qi falls on the right. Many people whom have a big stomach or have pains in their shoulders are all in some way related to this cycle. In the *Yi Jing* it describes this as "on the left hand side, there is a green dragon; on the right hand side, there is a white tiger." The green dragon is a metaphor for liver and is responsible for rising energy flows; whereas the white tiger is a metaphor of lung, responsible for falling energy flows. When this heavenly cycle is blocked, it will result in many bodily discomforts or health problems. To be connected with the cosmos' big energy field is the fastest method to help human beings to clear their meridian blockages and become healthy again.

When the human body changes in accordance with the Earth's orbit around the sun to complete a cycle (one year), it is called the 'big heavenly cycle'. It also means the human body Qi goes round the twelve meridian lines continuously. Our insides are in accordance with and connected with the outside. Our human body is connected by a web-like meridian system just like the Earth is with the star constellations, the galaxies and the cosmos. It is a web connecting physical reality, energy and consciousness. Even tiny changes in one locality of this web-like structure (see diagram below) will create an effect on the whole.

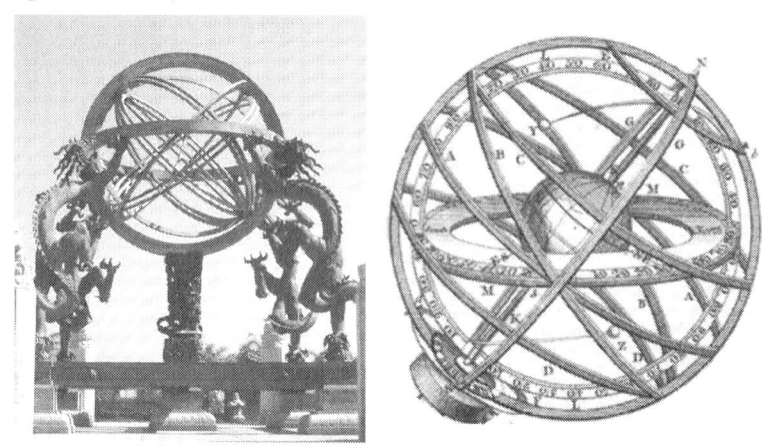

**Chinese Armillary Sphere**

However, if one only practices the upper Dantian to be able to channel spiritual messages, and neglects the practice of the lower Dantian, one will suffer from lack of physical stamina. For example, a person's hair will turn white earlier. In the West, some people practice how to channel, but never practice the movement of Qi circulating along the physical micro-cosmos of their meridian system. They often look very pale or overweight or suffer from serious health conditions. True Qi Gong practice looks after both the body and the soul, no more, no less. Practicing spiritual channelling but not the bodily Qi or vice versa are both deviating from the principle of 'heaven, earth and human as one'. If you only practice the lower part, just for the sake of improving physical strength, your soul will lack a sense of belonging. You will lack the ability to tell right from wrong and lose your direction in life. It is like a good car driven by someone who doesn't know where to go.

Internal alchemy is a key to open the secret door toward experiencing 'heaven, earth and human as one'. However, many people think that one has to go to the deep mountains in order to practice internal alchemy. In Chinese, the character 'immortal' (仙) is constituted by human (人) and a mountain (山). A modern interpretation of this might be that immortals live in the mountains and only by living in the mountains can you achieve

**Nei Jing Tu – Internal Alchemy**

Dan. This, however, would be a terrible misunderstanding. True internal alchemy treats the human body as a mountain (see picture on the previous page of the Nei Jing Tu). A person's spirituality or soul resides in the position of the heart and is therefore located in the deep centre of this 'mountain'.

The goal of internal alchemy is to develop the highest spiritual energy and ability of our human potential. Through conscious control of our six senses, we can blend in trainings and practices into our daily life. Every day, we can practice looking inwardly to self-examine our thoughts and behaviour. This is a method of distilling light energy. We also must be very keen to participate in our living and social environment, because we are all fundamentally connected and interrelated with one another.. There is no way we can train properly through total separation and isolation. It is the smelting and purification of the mind and the soul in the real world that counts. For instance, in daily life, we can practice how to let go of material comforts. People who develop this quality will improve faster.

In the *Dao De Jing*, Lao Zi writes about this practice in mundane life. He says, "The hermit can be secluded in the midst of crowds." This kind of practice is treating the Earth and human society as a big smelting furnace. We challenge and examine ourselves on a constant basis. Likewise, we will be able to then accumulate Dan and light on a constant basis. In a nutshell, we could say we first use our body to be the material basis of a smelting furnace. Second, the inward reflection and examination would help us to build up inner Qi. Then this Qi will in turn unclog the four major bodily channels and all the meridian pathways and points. In the end, through the Qi's movement inside the micro-cosmos of the meridian system, we will each reach our own revelation regarding the truth of nature and the macro-cosmos, and we will then experience being in the state of 'heaven, earth and human as one'.

# Chapter Three
# External Alchemy –
# One of the Forerunners of Modern Science and Technology

When we talk about alchemy or 'Dan', many peoples' first thoughts are of a magical golden drug, an 'elixir'. The notion is that, on taking such a drug, human beings would then become immortal. The theories, techniques and processes that produce this 'Dan' or 'elixir' is the purview of external alchemy. It seems that external alchemy is perhaps more widely known than internal alchemy. But in actual fact, the practice of internal alchemy as a path to immortality has a much longer history than the external one. After the Song Dynasty (960 - 1279), Dan practitioners realised the dangers of external alchemy as it involved the use of heavy metals that could be fatally poisonous. Therefore, they let Chinese pharmacologists take over and, over time, the drugs were refined and became an integral part of Chinese Medicine. An 'elixir' is sometimes used by people who have mastered Qi Gong to a very high level to perform a special kind of cleansing, called "using poison to eliminate poison". It, however, can only be applied at a certain stage of practice and the secret of this practice is only known by a very few people.

Nevertheless external alchemy, or the process of smelting natural minerals, was one of the forerunners of science and chemistry. It also led to the technological advancement of the smelting industry which invented such things as the metal alloy bronze, swords, mirrors, gunpowder and the compass, all of which have significantly contributed to human civilisation. In ancient times, the cauldron or 'Ding' (鼎) was designed to have three legs with each leg representing, in turn, heaven, earth and humans. The quantity and quality of the materials used also needed to be in accordance with the Qi field of the stars. Our ancestors believed that each star represented a deity. The equivalent of November in the Chinese calendar was considered as the best time to start a fire. In order to fully utilise the cosmic energy, the process must follow a full cycle of the sun, the moon or a star constellation (i.e. a small or big heavenly cycle). The person who is responsible for starting the fire must be very alert and experienced in observing and controlling the fire's temperature - for the right timing and the right temperature are critical skills in the process of Dan production.

The richness of the spirituality and technological sophistication involved in Dan smelting intrigued many famous ancient literati. During the Tang Dynasty, the so-called 'immortal poet' Li Bai (诗仙) wrote hundreds of poems that were related to Dan processes. Bai Ju Yi, another famous poet and important statesman who also lived during the Tang Dynasty, tried to learn the entire course of smelting Dan from Daoist masters.

'Dan sand' or Red Cinnabar is the basic material used to produce Dan. This is where the name 'Dan' originally came from. Dan sand is also called 'red sand' due to the red colour of the mineral. Its basic contents are sulphur and mercury. As early as the Stone Age, humans began to learn about and utilise Dan sand. Even in early times, Dan sand was somehow related to the notion of immortality. It is quite magical to obtain white or silver coloured fluid - namely mercury - from the red sand. Large quantities of mercury were used in many emperors' tombs even before the Qin Dynasty (221-206 BC). Therefore, the technology of using Dan sand to smelt for mercury may have been invented as early as the Warring States Period of Chinese History which began in $5^{th}$ Century BC. Before the Han Dynasty (206 BC – 220 AD), Dan sand and mercury were being used in external medicines.

Dan sand is a very light poisonous drug. For example, alchemist Chen Sheng used Dan sand with honey to create a drug that was said to have the effect of making people less hungry over the long-term. Although the taking of Dan sand can be slowly toxic, if used properly, it can be safe to use for medicinal purposes. In *The Classic of the Mountain and Sea* (山海经), the use of Dan sand and gold is mentioned many times. However, the book never states that taking these substances could turn people into immortals. Historically, men first of all wished to visit immortals living in faraway places to ask them for the method or drugs that would make them immortal. After such efforts failed, they turned to the practice of external alchemy using materials such as Dan sand.

One Classic Dan book from the Qing Dynasty (1644-1912) quoted Yi Jing Master Wei Bo Yang's words: "to avoid death, one needs to use Dan sand. When Dan sand is smelted in fire, it turns into mercury. It can be heavy or light. It is spiritual and mythical. It can be black or white, dim or bright. And it has all the attributes of the five elements." Later, there was a method developed called the yellow and white technique, which was the practice of smelting gold and silver.

External alchemy practitioners started to wake up from the intoxicating effects of the enchanting smoke from Dan smelting furnaces and the fascinating chemical reactions. This was due mostly to the severe toxic nature of these materials. They began to realise that relying on external materials to reach immortality was a mistaken path. Many Daoist elites began to use the process of smelting Dan as a metaphor to depict the actual process of cultivating high energy fields within the human body, i.e. the process of internal alchemy. The practice of internal alchemy reached its climax during the Tang (618-907) and Song Dynasties (960-1279).

To reiterate, the processes of external alchemy are where raw material such as Dan sand were refined into mercury through smelting at high temperatures and by following a series of sophisticated techniques. This external process was used to describe how human beings can use their own bodies to become the smelting cauldron, so to speak, and to refine their soul into higher energy fields. The make-up of the human body is far more complicated than the cauldron used for external alchemy. The principles however are the same. If you want to become gold, you have to be ready to be thrown into the smelting cauldron and endure the extreme pain of high temperatures. This is the only way heavy impurities can be dissolved and washed away, so that you then can become light and bright. In this Dan field, practitioners will start to radiate a beautiful purple light.

In my Qi Gong classes, once the whole class has entered into a deep still state, many students have reported to me that they have seen purple light in front of their closed eyes. Others have reported seeing golden, yellow light. I remember once a former patient of mine decided to join one of my Qi Gong classes as she had found my treatment to be quite effective and wanted to stay healthy. However, learning Qi Gong can require a substantial amount of time to be committed to practice. After a half day of meditation, when the group started to share thoughts and experiences, she asked: *"is it possible to invent a medication made of Qi so that we can just take it and be done with it? We would be healthy but without the hardship of practices."* This kind of thinking of seeking to rely on an external force to help us solve our problems is very popular nowadays. It has influenced all of us to differing extents and is a major obstacle to human evolution.

Before external alchemy became popular, *The Book of Zhuang Zi* recounted the following story whereby the Yellow Emperor asked Guang Cheng Zi about the Dao of longevity. Guang Cheng Zi told him: It must be quiet. It must be pure. It accumulates essence and stills the spirit. The method is called 'keeping to oneness'. It is said that Guang Cheng Zi used this method to cultivate his body and soul for 1,200 years and that his physical appearance did not grow old. This is internal alchemy. People ignore the good teachings of internal alchemy as they would rather seek outside help, such as Dan drugs, which ultimately led to the rise of external alchemy. It wasn't until the Tang Dynasty, when many emperors died of Dan poisoning, that external alchemy started to decline and internal alchemy practices rose once more and became even more sophisticated.

Today, China's economy is developing at a very fast pace. Peoples' living standards have improved dramatically and they've come to care more and more about their health. As a result, many medicines and supplements have poured onto the marketplace. Sometimes a very simple formula can cost more than gold. Furthermore, the product will sometimes have no effect whatsoever. However, some people will still blindly follow and believe in such products and continue to buy them. It makes me wonder that if this is a modern version of external alchemy; haven't we learnt enough from the past to see that blindly taking drugs can lead people to become weak, paralysed, and even lead to death?

Disaster is often the best teacher for human beings. In the history of Chinese medicine, there is a famous doctor by the name of Huang Pu Mi. He was the author of the most influential of the acupuncture classics *Zhen Jiu Jia Yi Jing (针灸甲乙经) or The Fundamental Principles of Acupuncture.* In his youth, he did nothing but fool around. By the age of 42 however, he caught a very serious disease and his whole body became numb. He turned weak and deaf and at the age of 52 he was poisoned after taking a Dan drug. He could not sleep at night. His bones were so painful that he tried to commit suicide. After all of this, he decided that he would learn Chinese medicine. He studied meridian theory, internal alchemy and went on to become a superstar in the field of acupuncture. His work is the classic of acupuncture that all practitioners, even to this day, must read.

External alchemy ultimately uses suffering to wake up human beings. For those who've tried or avoided training and practicing within themselves, but would rather rely on pills and drugs, the external pathway is definitely a dead end. Some wise, elite people have learned from their experiences and consequently have put more effort into practicing internal alchemy instead. As it was very difficult to explain the internal experiences such as describing the level of Qi and degree of energy required, it became common to use the vocabulary of some of the processes of external alchemy to help communicate these experiences. For example, internal practices can involve breathing that focuses on engaging Qi and temperature and is similar to that of using bellows to encourage a fire to start - the equivalent in internal alchemy is the heat within the body. It helps practitioners to use the same vocabulary and terminologies to pass on successful techniques. However, the use of external alchemy as a metaphor for documenting and recording has created many terminologies which are sometimes more confusing than clarifying.

Nevertheless, external alchemy has made important contributions to Chinese civilisation in giving birth to various smelting technologies. Its sophistication in terms of research and experimentation has reached very high levels. One of my friends has a Ph.D. in Material Science from an English university and was a top student at the Beijing University of Metallurgy. In England he led a research project that went on to receive an international award. When we talked about the achievements of ancient Chinese civilisation, he said that in ancient China, there was a kind of sword that was very thin and flexible. It could be used as a belt around the waist and it was so sharp that it could cut bricks and stones. Even with today's technology, we are unable to reproduce this kind of sword. We have lost the formula that can produce this special kind of steel.

The large and sophisticated equipment used to observe astronomy and detect earthquakes today are all benefits arising from the technology of external alchemy in ancient China. Many of the ancient Chinese scientists were Daoists whose early experiments with natural material involved the fundamental starting point of external alchemy - the smelting of Dan.

The route for human beings to seek immortality is from internal to external alchemy and back again. This is also the route for the improvement of our mind and soul, as well as the route for our civilisation to advance beyond materiality. We have to thank those emperors and aristocrats who died from the poison of external alchemy. They used their lives to teach us the lesson and led us to understand what the true Dao is. That is, our physical body is a smelting cauldron. It is the place where we 'cook medicines' for our own health. It is also where time and space, and life and death transformation takes place. In China, there is a saying, "three feet above you, there is a divine spirit looking after you". When you practice the light of Dan, you will be connected to the spiritual world. When you are connected to the spiritual world, you will be connected to a place beyond life and death. You will be able to travel around Earth and heaven, and experience your own immortality. **This Qi - this energy - has no nationality. Everyone has a Qi field that goes beyond being rich or poor - it makes no difference. Let us give up the excessive desire for money, fame, temporary satisfaction of material and sensual gratification and bravely walk toward the road of golden Dan.**

# Part Two

# Chapter Four
# The Earth Cauldron and the Fate of Men

Earth is our home. It is a living magnetic crystal sphere and an alchemical furnace that is constantly balancing both internal and external energy fields. Every single action taken in our daily lives is added to this Earth Cauldron. War, for example, is the largest source of waste and impurity that human beings are capable of creating. Other forms of human destruction and exploitation of the natural world include underwater nuclear explosions and natural gas extraction, to name just a couple. When such human behaviour interferes with the Earth's natural balance and harmony, upheaval and rising temperatures on Earth are bound to take place. It also leads to changes astronomically in, for example, the interrelated rotating movements between our sun and neighbouring constellations. Consequently, the natural environment that we rely on for survival is more likely to experience major turbulence.

Amongst the planets of the cosmos, our Earth is a beautiful garden. We often describe it as Mother Earth. Our existence totally depends on the light from the sun and on the water, air and minerals of the Earth, as well as its plants and animals. The conditions and changes that prevail on Earth directly determine the fate of us all. Therefore the pertinent question arises - do we want to be the gardeners, or the destroyers, of this beautiful planet? We human beings have already come to the edge. Our population has already exceeded what the Earth's resources can support, especially with our incessant demands in maintaining a high standard of living. In doing this we will only continue to exacerbate the scarcity of the Earth's natural resources, provoke further global warming, and lead to accelerated melting of the glaciers - these are just a few of the problems we are now facing.

We enjoy an immense vigour for life created by our capacity for free will. However, we have misused this gift from heaven and let it inflate our ego to such an extent that we have led ourselves astray and become incredibly greedy in the process. This greed will lead us to total catastrophe. All we need to do to recognise this is to open our eyes and reflect on recent world events. Examples include the ongoing global financial turmoil that was originally triggered by the United States' sub-prime crisis in 2007, the Boxing Day earthquake and resulting devastating tsunami in Southeast Asia and the Indian subcontinent in 2004, Hurricane Katrina that hit New Orleans in 2005, the 2008 Sichuan Earthquake, as well as recent epidemics such as bird flu, SARS, mad cow disease and Ebola.

What kind of warnings are we being given from these frequently occurring natural disasters and human failures? Shouldn't we stop for a moment to think: "Where are we going?" and, more importantly, "Where should we be going?"

The Maya were an ancient Mesoamerican civilisation that lived hundreds of years ago that mysteriously collapsed during the 8th and 9th centuries. They possessed the most accurate calendar system ever to be invented by mankind. Astonishingly, one of their calendar cycles known as the B'ak'tun ('Long Count' calendar) which lasts for 5,125 years, ended on the 2012 winter solstice. This calendar signified that we have completed a cycle of development and that a new era has begun.

According to one particular school of Indian yoga, in describing the cosmic changes that we are currently living in, human evolution on Earth is divided into four periods - the Golden Age, the Silver Age, the Bronze Age and the Iron Age. Today, we are living in this last Age, the Iron Age (the Kali Yuga in Hindi). In this Age, people's spiritual needs are suppressed and instead are focused on material needs. We are greedy and cruel toward each other. Even intellectuals and scientists are obsessed with materiality and lack respect for spirituality. We have forgotten the virtue of simple living, cooperation with others, and the wider common good. We do not do enough to protect our natural environment.

The Earth is currently going through a process of de-magnetisation. Consequently, large scale natural disasters could occur on a far more frequent basis. Many human lives could be lost. The Earth is effectively shaking away the old so that it can start over again. Human society is inside this huge Dan-smelting cauldron of planet Earth, and will likely experience more widely what we term global warming, earthquakes, volcanic eruptions, and so on. People who have trained in internal alchemy and obtained a high enough energy vibration characterised by golden and white light are better placed to endure any forthcoming ordeals and welcome in a new Earth and its next Golden Age.

According to ancient Daoist tradition, there are also records of cycles of human civilisations that have declined only for new ones to emerge. Disasters have always been the best teacher for human beings.

The sooner we as a global community awake the lesser the degree of potential destruction there will be. The cultivation of high energy vibrations through internal alchemy practices enables us to learn how to heal and improve ourselves. It will give us the confidence and strength to walk through the darkness of the lower energy levels of existence that are characterised by cruelty and self-destruction and thus enable us to rebuild our lives on Earth once again.

The question is whether or not we can be the masters of our own consciousness. If we can achieve this, then planets in other galaxies will also be able to evolve from lower animal lifeforms into species like ourselves that possess self-determination and the ability to create harmonious living environments.

The Findhorn Foundation is a very successful sustainable eco-community that has existed for over 50 years now. Located on the Moray Firth coast in Northern Scotland, it was founded by just three individuals. They first became known for growing award-winning vegetables out of what was an extremely barren wasteland. Some soil scientists came to analyse how this was possible only to be left thinking that there was some kind of 'x-factor' that they couldn't find. The community's founding ethos was not very different from that of a communist community - contribution based on capability, compensation based on need. It attracted people from all walks of life and from many different countries to come to work as volunteers. It gradually grew into a self-sustaining community with active units of production, construction, and education. It now offers multi-language education programs and is capable of hosting hundreds of people.

They pay a great deal of attention to spiritual practices. Many important contemporary figures in the field of spiritual practices have been invited to give seminars or speeches there. Driven by curiosity and the reputation of the Foundation and its community, I enrolled in one of their programs in November 2008. We arrived at a large mansion that is surrounded by acres of pine woodland. In the corridor, I saw bulletin boards that were full of program schedules and the room set up for registration was located in a huge sunlit ballroom. Many people, like myself, came from different countries.

The staff were very well organised, and they put into practice the principle of 'contribution based on capability, compensation based on need'. People who have financial resources will donate money to their cause and people who have no money will offer their services. The Foundation carries out various services that need support such as vegetable growing, cooking, cleaning, and teaching. Some volunteers and workers have experience in management or business and so will naturally be assigned duties within the internal management or organising guest reception and orientation, etc. There are both long term and short term volunteers and they can attend certain training courses free of charge. It is very similar to a work study program. People who believe in eco-community living and the harmonious development of our planet are brought together here. They are, in effect, purifying their souls here through selflessly contributing their skills, capabilities, wealth, and time.

How this community was started is the stuff legends are made of, but it is all true. Eileen Caddy and her husband Peter left managing positions at a large hotel in Forres, Scotland and began living in a small caravan in the nearby area with their young children. Through meditative practices Eileen started to hear a voice talking to her at night. This voice asked her to grow vegetables in a specific area of the caravan park where they were staying. She told Peter and Dorothy MacLean, a friend of theirs, about it, and without hesitation Peter and Dorothy supported the idea.

To cut a long story short, the end results were nothing short of amazing. That such a barren wasteland was able to produce an excellent harvest of vegetables, was nothing short of miraculous. They were able to create such bounteous crops because the voice and guidance they received had taught them how to change the quality of the soil and how to nurture the plants. Every time, when Eileen heard the voice, she would carefully write down what she heard and then tell the others. Sometime later, because their home had become crowded and noisy, she asked whether there might be somewhere for her to go for some peace and quiet. The voice replied and told her to go to a nearby public toilet so that she would be able to hear more clearly. So, she started going to this public toilet every night to continue to receive the important messages that were coming to her. The voice told her how to develop the place into a sustainable community and village. She, her husband and Dorothy all followed the guidance of the voice every step of the way and the vegetable crops grew better and better, bigger and bigger. More people gradually heard of this place in Findhorn and began to move there to live.

Another interesting anecdote concerns one of the earliest people associated with the Findhorn Foundation. This person lived in Edinburgh at the time and had decided to go for a walk in the botanical gardens there. Once there he chose to rest beside a large tree. As he sat there, quite still and relaxed, he looked off into the distance towards what appeared to be a small figure. At first he thought it was a little boy, but on closer examination he could see that this figure was not a human shape. The upper region was human-like but the lower part of him was more like the shape of a goat. It had little horns and a tail and a very pointy chin. This form is what's called, in English folk stories, a 'faun' which is very similar to a creature that is described in the classic Chinese book *The Mountain and the Sea*. This little faun was only about two feet high and it was curiously dancing around amongst the trees. As this person kept watching this little faun he noticed that it was gradually coming closer. It eventually came right over to where he was sitting and sat down in front of him crossing his legs. The man didn't have an idea what to do next and so simply leaned forward and said, "Hello." The little faun jumped, startled by the notion that this 'human' could seemingly see him. He replied "Can you see me?" and the man said, "Why yes, I can." "That's ridiculous, humans can't see us" the faun replied. And the man replied, "Well, it seems that some of us can!"

To make absolutely sure, the faun then jumped up, did a little dance on the spot and asked the man, "What am I doing now?" The man, of course, replied "You're dancing on the spot." The faun was now convinced that this man could indeed see him. It transpired that this faun was none other than the Greek nature deity known as Pan. From that moment on their conversations continued and they became great friends.

Almost forty years ago, the BBC broadcast a special program from the Findhorn Foundation. The host asked Eileen Caddy what this voice that she heard sounded like. Eileen said that it was just like a human talking to her but that the voice was somewhat faint. Interestingly, the community at that time had cleared a flat piece of land at the top of a nearby hill specifically for potential extra-terrestrials to land on. They sincerely believed that the success of their experiments and activities in agriculture and community building was a result of following the channelled guidance they were receiving from higher civilisations within the universe. Through meditative practices they became more aware that, in addition to Earth's civilisation, many other civilisations existed throughout the cosmos.

Human beings should strive to learn how to develop together with other cosmic civilisations to create a more harmonious cosmos. To achieve this, we need to start from a place of harmony within ourselves and with nature.

Many people think living in a temple is the best way to practice spirituality but, in fact, our body is its own temple. Our body is a pyramid. We do not need to rely on an external physical temple for spiritual cultivation. Our body is an extremely sophisticated biological 'super-computer'. It's an extremely effective and efficient vehicle that allows us to operate well in this world. You cannot begin to imagine how quickly it can synthesise and process complicated information. Some of the systems within our body have yet to be discovered by us. Spiritual cultivation, either via 'top down' or 'bottom up' practices (more on this in later chapters), enable us to realise our full potential. When more of our human potential is realised, the higher the energy levels we will be able to access (i.e. enter higher dimensions).

At the moment, human beings reside in the third and fourth dimensions. The distinctive faculties of each dimension can be briefly summarised as follows:

- In the third dimension a person is unable to communicate with other living forms existing in the cosmos. They cannot see or perceive various spirit forms.
- In the fourth dimension a person can travel to other planets. However they must rely on spacecrafts and/or high-tech communication devices to do so.
- In the fifth dimension the human spirit is able to take different forms and exist in multiple places on Earth simultaneously, i.e. a person's consciousness and body can be separated and appear in more than one place.
- In the sixth dimension the human spirit can access other spaces and galaxies; however, to do so, it must go through a space-time tunnel known as a stargate.
- In the seventh dimension the human spirit can go to other spaces and galaxies without the need to go through a stargate. They can go all the way to the centre of the cosmos. However, they must apply for permission before doing so. A person's capability for 'transforming into light' (虹化) in the higher realms is only possible by merging their spirit with an animal or plant form.
- In the eighth dimension the human spirit can travel to the centre of the cosmos freely without needing any permission.

What is 'transforming into light' (虹化)? It is a process that literally turns your physical body into light. Vibrating at a very high frequency can turn all materials into light and transform them into any form within the cosmos. It can form a human figure in the higher dimensions. In these higher dimensions the energy and density levels are different. The higher the energy and density level a person has, the more they are able to enter into the cosmic core where they will meet higher energy beings who take human form. Each dimension has its own laws and regulations. There are people on Earth who have cultivated themselves to such a level whereby they have been able to access as high as the seventh dimension. Indeed some scientists, artists and business people, both past and present, have been able do this.

Competition for survival is a natural instinct. Human self-awareness is a key to open up our heart's conscience. Our conscience gives us the ability to self-reflect. It is the guiding overseer of our consciousness. It assesses what kinds of thinking and actions are beneficial for our personal improvement as well as the harmonious and balanced development of integrating spirituality into our daily lives.

When conscience is not operating human beings exist at the lowest 'animal' level where the fight for survival leads to competition not only between themselves but also with their living environment. In the end, they run the real risk of wiping themselves out and destroying everything around them. The need to control, to possess to the point of greediness, to have excessive sexual desire can lead to power struggles and human atrocity. However, these instinctual energy fields can be creatively transformed into higher energy levels through the melting pot of internal alchemy practices where one can then cultivate the ability to enter higher dimensions. This is the process of self-preservation whereby a person is not only in a better position to safeguard themselves but is also better placed to protect others as well.

Success in spiritual practice needs both self-motivation and an external support system. The internal and external forces should be combined. There are different types of external help, such as seeking help from higher life forms and higher civilisations in the cosmos. One can practice to a level whereby you no longer need energy from the Earth, but rather absorb energy from the cosmos.

External forces from lower levels that are aimed at satisfying the human ego can not only be unhelpful for human beings, but can create a negative effect. So how do we distinguish between positive external forces and negative ones? The breadth and depth of our thinking will determine the quality of discernment.

To make a very simple point, what you eat can tell you who are. This means your choice of diet reflects the level of your energy field. For example:

> Primitive level: meat eater
>
> First level: fish eater
>
> Second level: vegetarian
>
> Third level: obtain energy from water
>
> Fourth level: obtain energy from light

The higher the level we reach, the less reliance there is on food. We, as humans, have the potential to live only on water and light. When human beings enter this level, we will live in a very advanced state of existence.

People who practice Qi Gong often say that humans are a micro-cosmos and so are directly related to the macro-cosmos of the Earth and the universe. The human body is connected by a web of nerve systems, blood vessels, a lymphatic system and a meridian system that carries out material and Qi exchanges.

Earth's magnetic lines work in the same way with an enormous web of universal energy always flowing and exchanging. Planets and constellations are also related via their orbiting rotations. Each is related and inseparable from all the others. We are living inside a physical web, an energetic web, and a web of consciousness.

The human body has many similarities when compared to the Earth. For example, the Earth has an axial magnetic line and many electromagnetic lines around it whereas the human body has a central meridian with many meridian lines around it. Also the Earth is a living magnetic crystal with the majority of its surface covered by water whereas about 60% of the human body is made up of water. When the quality of water in the human body is in good condition, the body itself becomes a beautiful crystal.

Within this holographic micro-cosmic, macro-cosmic structure, if just one element changes in either, it affects the other. That's why we say energy fields and information fields are not limited by national boundaries. If you think you can practice spirituality by shutting yourself down from the outside world by escaping to an isolated wonderland to meditate, you would be terribly mistaken.

In the past, Daoists lived in the depths of the mountains. They drank the mountains' spring water and were nourished by the winds and the rains. Their skin opened up to absorb light and Qi. The stones were their pillows and the caves were their shelters. The rise and fall of the sun corresponded with the rise and fall of the Dan inside them. This is what we call heaven and human as one. When these Daoist masters reached the Dan state, the fragrance of flowers would emanate from their bodies. They became immortals and travelled between the heavens and Earth.

However, in our modern times, we practice spirituality in the midst of pollution - polluted air, polluted humans, and polluted surroundings. As a small example, the construction materials of modern buildings are full of poisonous chemicals.

**Faced with the severity of our separation from nature, the question needs to be asked - is immortality still attainable?**

In the story of *Journey to the West*, the monkey Sun Wu Kong was thrown into Lao Zi's alchemical furnace where he burned for days. When he came out of the furnace, his eyes acquired a special quality and ability called "fiery eyes and golden pupils". We humans are currently experiencing being 'cooked' inside the giant alchemical furnace of planet Earth. Can we, like Sun Wu Kong, also expand our abilities and transcend time and space through the painful process of purification? Can we survive the ordeal, shake away our impurities and come out as gold – with renewed wisdom and enlightenment?

**The crises of the Earth and human society can be viewed as an opportunity for us. It is an opportunity to evolve beyond the boundaries of time and space, and upgrade to a higher level of humanity. It is a once-in-many reincarnated-lifetimes opportunity!**

# Chapter Five
# Why Doctors of Chinese Medicine Must be Able to Connect with the Divine

Chinese medicine is the only and most sophisticated traditional medicine system that is still alive and actively practiced in the world today. Chinese medicine embodies culture, medicine and science in one. It started even before written language arrived as primitive tribal people passed on early techniques such as stretching exercises, mind-directed movement of Qi, praying, stone acupuncture needles and herbal medicine. The knowledge and techniques accumulated for hundreds of years up to its prime period between the Warring States Period and the West Han Dynasty when the first great medicine classic *The Yellow Emperor's Classic of Internal Medicine* came into being. This book had comprehensively collected various schools of practice both before its time and at the time of its creation. The history contained within the book can perhaps be dated back as far back as the Stone Age.

Today our Earth is facing various crises including energy scarcity, increasing greenhouse gases, climate change, more frequent natural catastrophes etc. More than any other time in human history today's world needs the philosophies of Chinese medicine - the theory of 'heaven and human as one' - to find its way out from these precarious dangers. Chinese medicine knows how to conserve energy through the harmony between nature and human beings. It emphasises prevention of disease and maintaining good health through living a 'good' life (a very sophisticated theory based on "nourishing life") which could significantly save the cost of medical care both for the individual and wider society. It has irreplaceable advantages in both protecting our own wellbeing as well as, by extension, Mother Earth's.

The staying power and longevity of traditional Chinese medicine is due to its close relation to the theories and practices of internal alchemy. It is no accident that historically the most renowned internal alchemy masters were at the same time the most successful masters of medicine. Among them were Hua Tuo, Zhang Zhong Jing, Ge Hong, Sun Si Miao, Li Shi Zheng. The success of their medicine practice was a result of their internal alchemy achievements.

Our human body is internal alchemy's furnace. The heart is the fire as well as the place of spiritual light. To achieve Dan, fire is an indispensable factor. The saying goes, "The secret of internal alchemy written by all the alchemy books is all about the control of fire." Without fire, without spirit, the Dan cannot be created.

At the very beginning of the section *Ling Lan Secret Classics* in *The Yellow Emperor's Classic of Internal Medicine* it says: "The heart is the emperor's palace where spiritual light will appear. When the emperor sees things clearly, his subordinates will all be at peace and the world will prosper. If the emperor cannot see things clearly, the twelve departments underneath him will be in trouble. The pathways will be blocked and damage to the whole will take place." This means that a heart that is full of light that is fair and also selfless is the key to good health. At the same time it is also the key to a peaceful society, nations and the world at large.

*The Yellow Emperor's Classic of Internal Medicine* also says: "sages pass on spiritual messages, protect the Qi and connect to divine wisdom." Without being connected to the divine, the internal organs will become blocked, the Qi will disperse and death will follow. In other words, if one fails in internal alchemy, he or she will effectively become obsolete. It tells us very clearly that without practicing spirituality, without being connected to the divine, it isn't possible to keep your body healthy and live a long life.

Practicing spirituality is the practice of light - the Dan - of your heart. You need to open your heart, so that you will not get attached, become stubborn, biased or prejudiced. As a result, the range of your vibration or frequency will broaden. It is not unlike a cosmopolitan person who is more likely to be open-minded and less likely to be opinionated due to being well-travelled. It is easier and natural for this kind of heart to have the potential to merge with the bigger cosmos. When our ancestors described the infinity of the cosmos, they used the following description "the smallness that has nothing inside and the largeness that has nothing outside." For a Buddhist, it is called "complete perfection". For a Daoist, it is called "within the Dao, the Dao cannot be put into words because it is everywhere." Each cultural tradition has different expressions; the meaning, however, remain the same. It all points to one universal truth. The purpose of spiritual practice is to be enlightened about this truth.

It should be relatively easy to understand what the practice of the heart is. It includes working on your state of mind, to come to an understanding of a kind of love that embraces everything and everyone; we can term it 'big love'. This 'big love' is not only about loving your own self, but is about loving others too. Many people can think negatively when it comes to loving their own self. But in fact, if a person is incapable of loving himself or herself, this person will not be able to keep in balance his or her own Qi field; and therefore he or she will not be able to love others in the true sense of the word. If you have a low Qi field, you will not be able to help others, but rather others will end up helping you; essentially you will be draining other peoples' good Qi. In China, we sometimes use the expression "tapping into others' light", which means exactly that, given that our individual Qi fields are all interconnected. The waves and vibrations emanating from each of us are either reinforcing or depleting one another in a continual motion to find equilibrium. Therefore, for a person to truly love others, he or she must first purify himself or herself. They must first set their mind and Qi into balance.

In my personal experience over the years of clinical treatment and Qi Gong teaching, I have met many people whose minds are discontent or scattered, with resultant health problems that cannot be wholly resolved.

Once I had a woman come to my clinic who was a wife of a church minister. She complained that she always felt fatigued and that her whole body felt very uncomfortable. She had lots of aches and pains throughout her head and body. During the treatment, I came to the realisation that the cause of her suffering was that she had become very narrow-minded, and that she masked her inner feelings around others too much. For instance, she said that because she was the wife of a minister, she had to serve many people. She was very unhappy about this and kept on asking "What about me?", "What can I do for myself?"

As it turns out, she had, without realising, come to my clinic seeking psychological, rather than physical, treatment. A person is not going to evolve into a higher level of consciousness if they cannot let go of petty personal gains and losses. It is somewhat ironic that some people don't understand that, as Jesus said, "It is better to give than to receive." It was such a shame that as the wife of an influential minister, this woman did not realise the happiness that comes from giving. In the process of giving, our heart and soul will be lifted up by the energy of 'big love'.

We often hear parents talk about problems involving their children. One very common phenomenon I have observed is a parent's fear of losing their kids, and the tendency of giving more attention to their physical and material needs, rather than giving psychological and spiritual guidance. Fear is a kind of attachment. Kids will naturally not respond to this kind of low Qi field with respect. Instinctively, they do not want to be tied up by this low energy field and as a result, they may end up cutting off contact with their parents. Chinese parents will most often react to this kind of behaviour very strongly by accusing their children of not following the principles of filial piety - meaning that one should respect and take care of one's parents. Such a conflict and estrangement would escalate and the situation would lead everyone to feel intolerably heavy. However, if one wants to enter higher energy levels, one must let go of all fear and attachment. One must dare to stand up to question authority and traditional belief systems that gave rise to people's suffocation in the first place. To love someone is not merely the superficial action of giving them material and/or physical help; it is more important to help someone to progress spiritually.

When Chinese medical practitioners from the past talked about connecting with divine light (神明), they were decoding a secret heavenly truth. The Chinese word 'Shen' can refer to the ability to reflect and reveal the wider consciousness of the cosmos.

The 'spirit' (灵魂) talked about in Chinese medicine is closely related to the spiritual world (灵界), i.e. the wider consciousness of the cosmos. In Chinese medicine, they differentiate the concept of divine spirit and human spirit, and emphasise the need to be connected to divine light. Traditional Chinese medicine believes that the human body is a micro-cosmic open system that is connected with the macro-cosmos. There is a world of deities and immortals that are different and that exist in higher dimensions than the third dimensional world of human beings. Compared to human beings, deities and immortals are less confined by time and space. They exist in different forms and in different frequencies of vibration. They exist with much less attachment than human beings and are more transparent and light. Because of this, they are called divine light (神明). We human beings need to be helped and guided by these deities and immortals in order to evolve together with them into a higher state.

The process of being connected to divine spirit is part of the process of elevating the human spirit. In this process, one needs first to contact one's own divine teacher, mentor or guide so to speak. One of the masters of Chinese medicine, Zhang Zhong Jing once had to deal with widespread disease and epidemic in his home town. He had no previous clinical knowledge about this particular disease at all and therefore had no idea how to deal with it. He made a serious plea to the heavens to help him cure the villagers. One night, while seeming to be in a dream, he was visited by an immortal that proceeded to open his heart and place a shining golden book within it. When he woke up, he could feel a slight pain in his chest. From this experience, he found a way to cure people and moreover, he wrote one of the most important and world famous Chinese medicine classics *Treatise on Cold Damage Disorders,* the *Shang Han Lun* (伤寒论).

This divine teacher is also termed the 'external divine' (身外之神) in internal alchemy. When you have practiced to a level where your original spirit (元神) is properly nourished and your heart is in a state of stillness, you can wait for the 'external divine' to come and you will receive messages and be taught truths of the cosmos. It is a commonly held belief within Qi Gong and spiritual practice circles, that one can be taught by divine teachers. In Tibetan Buddhism there is this same tradition; the Daoists of internal alchemy also express this.

Within Daoist internal alchemy it is said, that only when you have surrendered yourself, to have let go of your consciousness of self or ego, to have become completely free from the interference and noise of thoughts, and have entered a state of stillness and tranquillity that you are then ready to experience the truth of the cosmos. The origins of the universe will unveil itself in front of your eyes. You will hear the voice of the divine and see images that you have never seen before. You will be enlightened and connected to the wisdom of the macro-cosmos. Once you have seen the truth of the universe, you would have left the darkness of unconsciousness for good. Your soul will experience a deep sense of belonging.

This is the same state we call 'heaven and human as one'. In this state of mind, you are not bothered by the triviality of worldly gains and losses. You will understand that to cheat others is no different than cheating yourself. You will realise there are many civilisations other than our human civilisation that exist in the universe and that we are all related. If we want harmony within the cosmos, we should start from the harmony inside of ourselves; only then will there be harmony between human beings and nature and, with it, the realisation of Dao in the universe. Our calling will then come from our heart and it is then up to us to immediately follow it and take action. Power is not derived from money and political authority; but rather it comes from the elevation of human life, from the understanding and practice of human spiritual evolution.

Channelling spiritual worlds is still very common in the UK. I have visited several channellers in my time here. However, most of them are channelling wandering earthbound human spirits rather than divine spirits in the macro-cosmos. These people are called mediums and they can help in communicating between living human beings and earthbound human spirits. For many, this ability came to them at birth, rather than via meticulous practices whereby the attainment of one's original spirit (元神) is achieved. Moreover, some of these mediums are often living in solitude or isolation sometimes in under-populated remote areas. Further, their mode of thinking tends to be directed outwardly which is an increasingly typical pattern in modern society. When all these lifestyle elements add up together, most of them can be quite unhealthy. No wonder a common image of channellers is often akin to that of pale faced witches. It can be said that the channels they receive are either limited or not very pure.

Another situation can also occur whereby the consciousness of the cosmos is mixed with human consciousness whereby a person is unable to distinguish one from the other. In such a case, a person might be very confused and appear to be pathological to others.

As is macro-cosmic law, human consciousness is intricately connected. Being attached means being firmly held by a particular type of consciousness. If held by materialism, it will lead one to believe that what the five senses perceive is the only truth of the world. This is the most common fallacy or mythology of our modern time. We have abandoned spirituality and its pathway to immortality that is originally imprinted in all of us. Instead, we are deeply deceived and entangled by our ego, which locks our heart from opening to our fullest potential. The greed towards material wealth and the low energy field of ephemeral pleasures drag us down and forbid us from seeing the truth and origins of the cosmos. When people are so entrenched in this kind of Qi field and way of thinking, it can then be very hard for them to dig themselves out.

Outside of the visible light and the vibration of the visible physical world there are many invisible carriers of information. There are wandering human spirits, spirits of past wise men and women, past enlightened masters such as Buddha, or the immortals of the macro-cosmos that have never incarnated into human form, and so on. To be connected with the large wisdom of the macro-cosmos, you need to practice to a certain level where the quality and purity of your heart and physical Qi vibration can allow you to emanate light.

As was quoted in a previous chapter, "Three feet above your head, there is a divine spirit watching you." Internal alchemy which leads to the cultivation of Dan light will ultimately connect you to this divine spirit. From there you can then gain access to the macro-cosmos. The macro-cosmos is not only a field of energy, but also a field of information. When you are in this higher consciousness state, you are beyond death and you can travel freely within the cosmos. The issues of diseases and health are then no longer a consideration or problem.

We human beings are entering a higher evolutionary stage. This divine wisdom, or the big wisdom of the cosmos, is the manifestation of the higher civilisations' consciousness. If you will, imagine it as the 'supercomputer of the cosmos'. This supercomputer can perform calculations and information processes of all the details within the universe at an amazing ultra-high speed. These divine beings are travelling at the speed of photons or faster. They can decode everyone's thoughts as every thought has a frequency. The composition of your thoughts will speak for themselves regarding the level of your energy field and the degree of purity of your humanity. The difference of one thought can be the difference between heaven and hell. Even if you shut your doors, you cannot hide from their view. Even from far out in space they scan everything that is happening on Earth. However, they will not interfere with us. Nevertheless they are watching us very attentively because they know we are an inseparable part of them, that we are part of the whole. The difference is that they are, so to speak, standing higher up on the mountain and therefore have a broader view and the ability to see things more objectively without attachment and limitation. The information they have is therefore more accurate.

Given our limitations we can hardly imagine what they are capable of, let alone understand the level of their sciences and technology. However, when connected with this 'supercomputer' we can draw on its wisdom, knowledge and information to deal with our difficulties, challenges and dilemmas, and furthermore, to give up ego and evolve into a higher level. The principle, or the password, to this cosmic supercomputer is 'fairness, selflessness and to be as transparent as light' (正大光明).

The tradition of 'fairness, selflessness and to be transparent as light' had great influence on the ancient Chinese rulers' decision-making processes throughout all dynasties. The teacher of the countries ruler had on many occasions been a Chinese doctor. For example, the teacher of the Yellow Emperor was a Chinese medicine doctor called Qi Bo. There was a Chinese saying that said, "The superior medical doctor manages the country." These Chinese doctors as advisers to the ruler would always encourage living in harmony with the Dao of the cosmos.

If you want to be connected with the divine you need to have a very light and pure Qi. At the same time, you should not be afraid of the rigorous trials that come with the cultivation of internal alchemy. For example, only through a painful self-examination process can people recognise and release their ego, and let go of their emotional and intellectual burdens. Unfortunately, some people have to wait until a terminal illness before they can come to this kind of realisation.

In 2001, I guided a Qi Gong tourist group to visit China, going to the famous Daoist Mountains for retreat and Qi Gong training. In the group, there was a masseuse who suffered from a minor case of high blood pressure. When we arrived at Jade Dragon (Yu Long) Mountain in Yunnan Province, we reached to 4,600 metres above sea level when she suddenly fainted. To begin with everybody thought that it was caused by a lack of oxygen and she was therefore treated as such. However, when we came down from the mountain, she kept having the same problem and her heart and breathing stopped several times and she lost consciousness. Because she had effectively been poisoned by western medicine in the past, she insisted on being treated by Chinese medicine only. When we reached Kunming, the capital of Yunnan, we took her to the city hospital where they found her heart muscle was lacking a sufficient supply of blood. Through the application of Qi Gong, acupuncture and IV treatments, she regained her consciousness. She went on to tell me her experiences while unconsciousness. She said that her spirit went out of her body and that she saw her deceased uncle. Her uncle told her, "you must go back and your health will improve." Magically, after this near death experience, she acquired the ability to diagnose diseases through observing patients' auras.

People often acquire special abilities after near death experiences and this has been recorded in many places and dates back to very early times. The near death experience of this woman led her to make some life altering decisions. As soon as she went back home, she ended her marriage that was, to all intents and purposes, finished a long time ago. She realised that she wasn't being true to herself. Her heart had been sending messages over and over again until it had almost stopped functioning. However, in her near death experience, she got the message that her time had not yet come.

After this experience, whenever we spoke on the phone, she would be able to tell me what kind of light was surrounding me. Sometimes it was purple light, other times it was golden light. Despite the fact that she lives in Canada and I am either in China or the UK, now that she had passed her trial and relinquished her burden, she is now capable of seeing light no matter how far the distance. She continues to help people to improve their Qi field through them using their own Qi and light energy. Later on, she found a new partner and started a happy new life. What a powerful experience of rebirth this was, led by a connectedness with a spirit in the form of her uncle.

There are quite a few people who have experiences of communicating with spirits. Some are closer to us, i.e. they are more approachable and can give us more specific and more actionable guidance. However, the higher order immortals of the cosmos tend to be more objective, strict and severe, because they are standing higher and farther away and are therefore seeing a larger picture and are closer to the truth. For instance, from a more macro and long term view, the higher order immortals will understand the necessity of certain suffering and setbacks, so long as the latter can give rise to greater awakening and benefit the long term growth of the universal consciousness.

The true love of human beings by these divine spirits is encouraging the latter to go through the painful trials and challenges so that they may attain a higher level of being.

Chinese medicine has a similar deep understanding of human suffering. Their treatment approach is not to eliminate the symptoms, but rather to view any painful symptoms as part of the natural healing process. For example, the processes where the human body and mind are going through self-rearrangement. To be connected with the divine is also about heaven and human harmony or oneness. This harmony is a balanced state, as well as a dynamic balancing process. Specifically, there is a positive force and a negative force. When the positive and negative forces are equal, equilibrium or harmony is reached. Therefore pain is the process of finding the equilibrium once again. The process of reaching a state of equilibrium is the process of the redistribution of energy. Some will continue to live and some will die. This is the necessity of pain and loss in the process of living and creating new life.

In today's world, there are many people who are drained through addictions to material gratification. This is a very low energy field and it has the potential to ruin our Mother Earth. The Earth, in order to regain its state of equilibrium, may have no choice but to take action against this low energy field. The law of nature has to remain in place to keep itself in balance. Earthquakes and volcanic eruptions are like spontaneous Qi Gong movements of the Earth. Their purpose is to shake away the unbalanced, unsuited energies so that the Earth can settle into a new equilibrium. Our body is a living entity, so too is the Earth, and so are the other planets in the cosmos. From infinity's point of view, one hundred thousand years is no different from one second. An evil person's rule compared to that of the timeless living consciousness of the cosmos is always short lived.

# Chapter Six
# An Overview of Daoist Internal Alchemy

There are many different schools of ancient Daoist practice. In this chapter, I want to provide a glimpse into some of the different practices that exist within these schools.

There are five sections to this chapter:
- The Nine Methods of Daoist Initiation and Orientation of the Dragon Gate Lineage
- The Practice of Daoist Inner Alchemy (Dan Dao)
- Heaven and Human Creating Together (Tian Ren He Fa)
- Daoist 'Cultivation of Truth' Practice
- A Short Glossary of Daoist Internal Alchemy

They all involve very systematic methods of cultivation. The subtlety and sophistication of them go beyond words. They follow very esoteric teaching patterns instructed by sage-level teachers who have and still do operate apprenticeship systems. The teaching is tailored to each individual's energy but they also have a general pattern and practice which I will endeavour to illustrate here, some of which are only kept within each lineage's teachings. **Please note that this is for illustrative purposes only and is not designed as a practical step by step teaching.**

# The Nine Methods of Daoist Initiation and Orientation of the Dragon Gate Lineage

### 1st Method: Self-Reflection And Getting Rid Of Bad Habits

**Practices:**

| | |
|---|---|
| Step 1: | Self-reflection in a dark room for two months. |
| Step 2: | Sit in lotus posture in a dark room for two months. |
| Step 3: | Sit in lotus posture in a room for two months. |

**Purpose:** To drive away desire and quiet down the mind and soul. To let the conscious mind calm down into a peaceful state.

**Posture:** Imitate nature, adopt the lotus position.

**Rationale:** To understand where human beings come from. Human beings come from emptiness and return to emptiness.

**Result:** Gain deep comprehension of the true meaning of the origins of the cosmos.

### 2nd Method: Calming The Mind, Rehabilitating The Heart & Nourishing The Spirit

**Practices:**

| | |
|---|---|
| Step 1: | Light incense, sit in lotus posture in a basement and practice the 'mind power method'. |
| Step 2: | Sit in lotus posture in a suspended box and practice how to focus the mind and soul. |
| Step 3: | Sit in lotus posture in a cemetery and practice how to keep the mind and soul calm and still. |

**Purpose:** To know the difference between innate and acquired human intelligence.

To apply intelligence in order to understand the different dimensional layers of the cosmos.

To progress from logical, abstract and imaginary thinking and evolve into intuitive thinking and then use this to understand the cosmos and its structure.

To develop the depth and width of the intellect - focused mind and soul.

To practice self-control of one's intellect - keep a calm and still mind and soul.

**Rationale:** To understand the world we live in has different dimensions, i.e. the truth of the cosmos.

To gain a deep understanding of the meaning of the theory 'three dimensions of the world'.

## 3rd Method: Mortification Practice Of The 'Three Dimensions Of The World'

**Practice of Step 1 (The Lower Layer):**

      Between humans - practice spirit

      Between humans and objects - practice Qi

      Between humans and animals - practice consciousness

      Between humans and plants - practice essence

      Between humans and the deceased - practice soul

**Purpose:** To understand the nature of the relationship between humans and other entities.

**Practice of Step 2 (The Middle Layer):**

Practice with the moon, the sun, and different aspects of the cosmos, the inner relationships of which are very wide and delicate.

**Purpose:** To observe the pattern of movement of the sun and the moon reflected in the human body. Here, the practitioner's concept of time and space will change.

**Practice of Step 3 (The Star Constellations):**

Practice with the North Star (the Big Dipper) and the eight hexagrams (the I Ching's Ba Gua)

Practice with the rest of the star constellations.

Practice with objects of form, as well as the vibrations of the formless.

**Purpose:** To obtain immense energy and power and to develop the ability to do things that are beyond the limitations of time and space.

## 4th Method: Fasting

**Practices:**

Step 1: Stop eating carbohydrate food.
Step 2: Stop eating all food and discover the hidden apertures and spaces of the inner organs.
Step 3: Hold stillness – from life to death.

**Purpose:** Cleansing the body to return to the foetus state, to freely control life from the beginning.

## 5th Method: To Become A 'Living Dead' Person

**Practices:**

Step 1: Create your own grave, and pray to your spirit to protect yourself.

Step 2: Reflection - sit in front of water or a mirror and watch the self very attentively.

Step 3: Thoroughly understand the spirit of Yin and Yang's subtleties.

**Purpose:** When people come back to life from a near death experience they understand the following:

1. Self-trust
2. Self-protection
3. Human beings are not perfect, so they need to make every effort to improve
4. Where I come from, why I came here, where I will go back to and what I should do?

## 6th Method: Cultivation Of The Dao To Build Foundation

**Practices:**

Step 1: Basic level foundation building practice: cultivate the inner body – flesh, tendons, bones and muscles of the body. Engage relationships, events and objects with three dimensional thinking.

Step 2: Middle level foundation building practice: the practice of essence, Qi, and spirit (Jing, Qi, Shen) that are both inside and outside of the body (heaven, Earth and human) i.e. the relationships between human beings and the celestial levels.

Step 3: Upper level foundation building practice: to practice the origin of essence, origin of Qi, and origin of spirit beyond time and space in order to understand the life cycle of the living cosmos.

**Purpose:** Adjusting essence, Qi and spirit (Jing, Qi, Shen).

To develop different states of consciousness and to understand the different dimensional layers of the cosmos.

Better manage the multiple relationships between you and your environment.

## 7th Method: Expanding Wisdom

**Practices:** Cultivate five skills:
1. Human Life Patterns - The study of human life patterns from birth through until death.
2. Predictions - Predicting developmental trends and direction of fate.
3. Face Reading - Studying the external image to understand peoples' inner nature.
4. Medicine - Methods that can relieve the unfortunate suffering of fate.
5. Mountain - The study of the methods and techniques developed in the mountains that can master fate – *For extended details of this*

*practice please see appendix B at the back of this book.*

**Purpose:** These five skills are used to connect humans, Earth and heaven together. The *Book of Changes* holds the truth about humans, Earth and heaven. It describes the most fundamental theory, whereas the five skills are the practical applications of this.

These five skills are based on the Dao and use practical applications to support the Dao, to save people, to carry on the Dao and disseminate the Dao. If the Dao can be kept, the human mind will become enlightened. The higher the Dao state, the higher the techniques.

## 8th Method: Cultivating The Spirit (Shen)

Cultivating the spirit (Shen) has the following aspects:

**Consciousness (Shi Shen):** practice multi-dimensional thinking so that one can deal with worldly issues based on deep and clear understandings of these issues, i.e. examining them from different levels and different perspectives to help solve problems. There are three levels and nine different methods.

**Original Spirit (Yuan Shen):** Sometimes referred to as the subconscious. This is when consciousness calms down and the original spirit rises to the surface.

When the Yin spirit comes out, it is experienced with irregular dreams or hallucinations, such as views of flowers, grass, plants, mountains and rivers, gardens and pagodas. After persistent practicing of tuning in, the above state and vision will become more regular. One can inwardly visualise his or her own internal organs, bone structures, meridians and blood system. Control of consciousness is required to do this.

Continuing the practice into a deep state will allow one to see many visions. When the Yin spirit is practiced well, one will enter a very still and quiet state – a no-mind state. When this practice of the Yin spirit is completed, the Yang spirit will then appear. A very lively 'baby' will come out and travel around the whole body. At the beginning it will be hard to control the baby's movement in that it will suddenly move up or down, sometimes left, sometimes right. However, through the deepening of the practice this tricky baby will begin to follow the commands of the practitioner, i.e. moving inside or outside of the body, up to heaven or down into the Earth. When the practitioner gains this level of freedom, it means his or her Yang spirit training is complete.

Once the practice of original spirit is completed, the practitioner will be in a very still and quiet state, and can wait for the external immortal spirit to come and give him or her heavenly orders and information.

**Cultivating Spirit (Lian Shen)**: In essence, whether cultivating Yin or Yang spirit, it is a process from formless spirit to a spirit that takes form, from spirit without substance to spirit with substance, and from irregular to regular access of spirit.

## 9th Method: Bathing

**Medicine bath:** To get rid of impurities from the body; to optimise the body and to stimulate its potential.

**Earthly bath:** To embrace the moisturising and nurturing of nature's substances, such as rain, snow, fog, dew, etc.

**Heavenly bath:** To embrace the nurturing of celestial bodies.

**Formless and on-substance bath:** To accept the moisturising and nurturing of formless non-substance.

# The Practice of Daoist Inner Alchemy (Dan Dao)

## **Preparation Before Practice:**

1. Body cleaning: using warm water, clean the genital area and perineum and then warm the area with steam water. Clean this area every time before sitting meditation.
2. Empty the bowel and bladder.
3. Begin to calm the mind and sit.

## **The 1st Step: Building The Foundation – Practice Essence To Qi**

**Aim:**  Generate heat and set up the furnace (to turn essence to Qi needs heat)

**Method:**  Concentrate on the lower Dantian and perineum. The state of the mind needs to be neither in total concentration nor totally absent but rather to be relaxed and neutral yet present. The true baby yang time is indicated for men when, at a deep relaxed state of non-thinking the penis becomes erect. Once this occurs there needs to be a focus towards the perineum point without any generation of mental thought. From here, wait until the internal essence begins to develop strength. When the sensation similar to that of ejaculation arises take that sensation and bring it within yourself, relax into it and it will transform into essence (sometimes referred to as medicine) for the body.

Make sure not to leak or release this essential medicine. The heart will receive the medicine. Keep awareness in the heart and breathe. For men, the penis will become soft. The heart will experience a very strong comforting sensation. After half an hour, it will feel like you've become a brand new person. Close the eyes and keep to this state.

The characteristics of successful 'foundation building' are:
- The fullness of essence will lead the person to feel very content, i.e. have no desires or lust of anything in general, sex in particular.
- There will be no discharges of sperm or vaginal fluid and the penis will not become erect.

*Note: In general, to reach desireless contentment: Men need three years and women need one and half years of practice.*

## The 2nd Step: Practice Of The Heart – Practice Converting Qi To Spirit (Shen)

### Formulating the Small Cosmic Orbit:
**a)    The Vertical Water – Fire Exchange:**

The water and fire elements vertically exchange between the heart (fire) and the kidneys (water). A person's in-born Qi (Yuan Qi) will automatically form a small orbit. The route of this small orbit is from a point between the two kidneys 'Ming Men' (命門) going up the back (but in front of the spine) to a point at the lower apex of the heart 'Jiang Gong' (绛宫). Then from the heart going back down the front of the body to return to the space between the two kidneys. The Qi needs to circulate around this route 36 times.

Later on, the Qi does not rotate around the small orbit, but simply moves directly between the heart and kidneys up and down for 36 times.

Later still, without the up and down movement, the warm Qi from the kidneys will begin to rise to the heart. The heart and kidneys begin to exchange directly between one another. The distance between the heart and kidneys, in effect, reduces and when they become one, internal alchemical medicine is produced.

### b) The Horizontal Wood – Metal Exchange:

The exchange between the liver (wood) and Lung (metal) elements is a horizontal exchange through the Belt Meridian or (Dai Mai). The liver Qi and lung Qi exchange by moving around the body starting from the navel, going right, then to the back, round to the left, returning to the navel and continuing in this horizontal clock-wise rotation 36 times.

## Formulating the Big Cosmic Orbit:

### The route of the big cosmic orbit is as follows:

Perineum (Qi Xue/炁穴) → Tailbone (Wei Lü/尾闾) → Lower Back (Jia Ji/夹脊) → Base of the Neck (Yu Zhen/玉枕) → Top of Head (Kun Lun Ting/昆仑顶) → Third Eye (Ming Tang/明堂) → Tip of Nose (Bi Zhu/鼻柱) → Tongue to the upper palette (Shang He Qiao/上鹊桥) → Lungs (Twelve Chong Lou/十二重楼) → Heart (Wu Zang Liu Fu/五脏六腑)→ Navel (Qi/脐) → Lower Dantian (Xuan Guan/玄关) → Perineum (Qi Xue/炁穴)

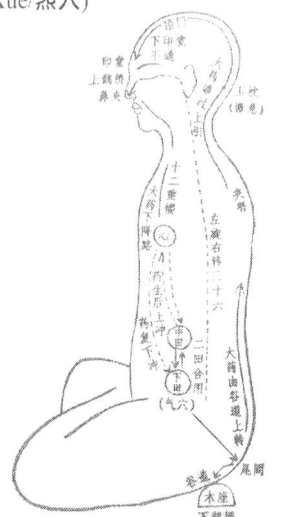

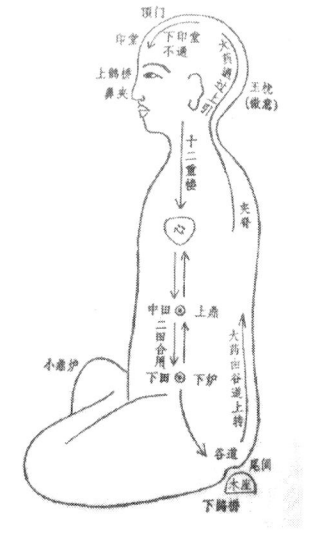

**Route of the big cosmic orbit 天线路**

Regarding the three points on the back, the first one Wei Lü is located on the third vertebrae at the junction between the Ren and Du meridians, the second Jia Ji is located on the spine of the lower back region and the third Yu Zhen is located on the twelfth vertebrae on the neck area. When these three points/gates open, the Qi will rise up to the head and circle for 81 cycles.

When Wei Lü opens up, the feeling is akin to the whole pelvis area seemingly disappearing, and the warm Qi goes up along the Du meridian. The Qi will stop at Jia Ji and Yu Zhen for a while before reaching the top of the head. If something occurs here, you need to stay quiet. If the Qi does not go down, you can use your awareness to show the way by contracting your eyebrows and opening and closing your eyes nine times.

To open the big cosmic orbit, one must practice being inactive, i.e. awareness/consciousness will not lead the Qi. After opening, consciousness should not rotate around the big cosmic orbit, but around the small cosmic orbit. The Qi should rotate clock-wise 81 times around the top of the head.

In so doing, the Ren, Du and central meridian will become one. The Qi will go up and down and around the whole back and chest. The body will become warm. The Qi will fill both the back and the front. This is the stage where the big cosmic orbit is realised which is also called obtaining the Dao. At this stage, you enter 'foetus breathing'.

After the big cosmic orbit has opened, you will automatically want to take a bath four times a day. The Qi will come at Zi (sunrise), Wu (midday), Mao (sunset), and You (midnight). Heavy and dirty Yin Qi in the body should be washed off. The Qi will come regardless of whether one's consciousness calls for it or not. The warm and joyful feeling will gradually swamp the whole body. During these moments, you want to be both motionless and speechless.

## The 3rd Step: Inaction To Return To Emptiness – Foetus Breathing To Return To The Dan

**Aim:** To form golden Dan. To form the foetus and then leave the foetus.

**Method:** Foetus breathing to return to the Dan. Nourishing and inaction to return to emptiness.

The purpose of internal alchemy is to cultivate the essence, Qi and spirit of the human body and distil them into concentrated Qi. Internal alchemy is formless. However, it can create heat, light, euphoria, or a sense of expansion. There are several hundred different types of Dan, which can be roughly categorised into high, medium and low quality types.

The forming of the Qi foetus begins at the second step and is completed here at the third step. When the foetus is completed, you can see an internal light and also see into your internal organs.

When forming the Qi foetus and entering foetus breathing, a sensation of warmth can be felt within the whole body without, however, experiencing Qi moving up and down or rotating. One will also stop normal external breathing through the nose and mouth and enter into a still and quiet state with no interference of any thoughts. Meanwhile, the Qi is moving automatically. Furthermore, the soul is alert and consciousness is in charge.

During foetus breathing the practitioner is in a deep state of stillness. The Qi of the entire body stops moving. One feels nothing, stops using consciousness to keep still and loses any sense of self or other concepts. Sitting in such a deep state four times a day each day for just 20-30 minutes can add on thirty years of longevity to a person's life.

Foetus breathing is the dividing line between being immortal and mortal. After completing foetus breathing, the body becomes pure Yang energy. The whole body will be immersed in a warm heat 24 hours a day every day. Therefore, one will no longer feel the need for actively bathing in the four time slots any more (Zi – Wu – Mao – You).

At the beginning of forming the foetus, the spirit is still Yin and is called Yin spirit. The Yin spirit will turn into Yang spirit once the foetus is complete. When the foetus is complete, white hair will turn black again, lost teeth will grow back, external breathing will stop and addictions and desires will fade away.

After the foetus is complete, you can then choose to leave the foetus, i.e. the soul can leave the body. In order to do that, you have to meet the following requisites:

1. The whole body's Qi is fully charged.
2. Major meridians are all opened, hundreds of small meridians are all opened and Qi can go anywhere throughout the meridian system.
3. To be in an absolute still and quiet state.
4. The soul cannot leave from the kidneys, rather it must leave from the top of the head.

# Heaven and Human Creating Together (Tian Ren He Fa)

Through internal alchemy, we can understand the holographic nature of the cosmos – From 'heaven and human as one' to 'heaven and human creating together'.

Human beings are connected to the cosmos through four channels:

1. Digestive channel - the digestive system.
2. Air channel - the respiratory system.
3. Skin pores channel - The Qi exchanges between inner and outer via the skin pores of the whole body.
4. Central meridian channel - it is through this channel that human beings can absorb large volumes of Yang spirit energy. However, it has to be developed through practice. It is the channel to nourish Dan and original spirit and it is the Yang channel of 'Chong Ju' (foetus releasing channel), i.e. where the 'light baby' flies out of the body to travel into the cosmos.

The shared function of these four channels is to ensure that human beings and the cosmos are constantly exchanging energy in order to keep the human body full of vitality. The first two channels have been thoroughly investigated and understood by modern science. The latter two channels however have regressed to a dysfunctional state among normal people. Historically practitioners of internal alchemy, in transforming their lives, practiced collecting Qi, accumulating light and forming Dan to nourish the foetus. Through this process, they searched for ways to open up and maintain these two latter channels.

The skin pores of living organisms were a more primitive channel existing long before the digestive and respiratory channels. Early single cell organisms had no internal cavities. The energy exchange between these organisms and the cosmos relied entirely on the surface pores of the cell. However, with the evolution of living organisms, internal cavities appeared in which sophisticated organs and systems came into being with divisions of digestion to receive nutrition, and respiration to receive oxygen. The exchange function of skin pores gradually regressed. However, with close observation, normal people can still discover that their skin pores do exchange Qi with the environment even though the amount of exchange is extremely limited. With internal alchemy practice, the regressed skin pore channel can be stimulated to re-open in a reasonably short period of time.

The opening of the central meridian, however, often relies on the support of an enlightened teacher. The central meridian needs to get the Qi all the way through and sometimes requires to be rebuilt by strong force. It is, so to speak, the 'super-highway' whereby human beings can be directly connected and merged with the energy field of the cosmos. It is the 'shortcut' gateway of internal alchemy and is called the 'middle yellow' method, or 'sudden enlightenment' in ancient times.

The following methods can assist people today to re-open the third and fourth channels (i.e. the skin pores and the central meridian) that have been closed for so long.

**Practice methods:**

> Heart and soul practice – constantly remind oneself of the following four concepts:

1. All living things, including seemingly lifeless physical objects (e.g. stones), are constantly sending signals and waves of information out into the cosmos.
2. The Qi in the human body is a conscious vehicle for sending and receiving information.
3. The purple, white and yellow lights people see under Qi Gong states are energy sources filled with consciousness and power.
4. The Qi sent by powerful thoughts that have strong intention have no limitations in time and space.

The goal of heart and soul practice is to totally dismantle the confines of third dimensional reality as well as rational experiences and concepts, so that the doors toward the actual practice of invisible universal higher orders can be opened. Further robust practices are required in order to stimulate and open up the skin pores channel and the central meridian channel.

For example, the emphasis of some methods, such as Qian Cheng Gong's nose point method, 'hearing skin' method and 'expansion and contraction' methods, are to stimulate and re-open the regressed skin pores channel. Still, the emphasis of others, such as the Qian Cheng's Gong's 'opening the central meridian' method, 'seven wheel secret mantra vibration' method and 'central meridian rotation' method are opening up, expanding and rebuilding the tightly closed central meridian channel.

Normally the average person, after two to three months of practice, can begin to use these two channels. These two channels, in turn, will readily receive Qi and light that are needed in internal alchemy and, in so doing, a person will attain special faculties in merging with the cosmos - 'heaven and human as one' - that are beyond ordinary peoples' imaginations.

These special faculties include:

1. Keeping a better controlled connection between the heaven and human energy fields which will help maintain more balanced life energy.
2. The human energy field can send out, receive and process information from the cosmos. Research has proven that the human brain can be an extremely powerful supercomputer for highly experienced internal alchemy practitioners.
3. The human energy field can tap into the cosmic energy field. Successful internal alchemy practitioners can mobilise the super energy of the cosmos to perform remote viewing, distance healing, and remote energy giving. They can create the direct effect of 'heaven and human as one' as if there are no intermediary processes (when usually there are).

'Heaven and human creating together' is a form of heaven and human resonance practiced by internal alchemists. It is a qualitative heightening of ability once the accumulation of universal energy has reached a very high level. In this circumstance, a thunderous sound can be heard from the practitioner's body. His or her life is purified by water and fire in order to transmute into a higher form. In fact, this is the phenomenon of crashing the gate and opening the point, created by the enormous power released by the vibrational resonance of the human and heaven energy fields. The resonance of the heaven and human energy fields and 'heaven and human creating together' is a landmark achievement of each internal alchemist.

There are two ways to reach this level. One is the gradual route, i.e. to practice the small and large cosmic orbit one step after another, and to pass through each gateway one after the other. This practice takes quite a long time.

The second way is the aforementioned 'middle yellow' method. It uses the Ling Zang style of the foetus breathing technique, through very active means to accumulate energy. It will be guided by the 'light baby' that is 'birthed' through the practice. The core aim of the technique is the effortless merging of Qi and light stored in the central meridian. Through the continual purification of the heart and spirit and constant charging energy from the cosmos, the Yin and Yang undergoes dynamic interaction, which will quickly thrust the resonant vibration of the 'heaven and human energy fields', resulting in 'heaven and human creating together.'

# Daoist 'Cultivation of Truth' Practice

Most Daoist schools' Qi Gong practices include the following four aspects:

1. **<u>Xing (Spirit) and Ming (Body) Practices That Are Cultivated Simultaneously</u>**

**Xing Gong:** spirit, soul, will, tranquillity, stillness
**Ming Gong:** Qi, blood, essence, tendons, bones, skin

To practice Xing (Spirit) Gong is to understand the different spirit dimensions and the capabilities within different levels of consciousness. Based on the mastering of ordinary capabilities, one can develop potentially extraordinary capabilities. To do so is to search for the dynamic equilibrium of the human body through confronting and resolving the inner and outer pressures found therein, and to discover the connection between human nature and the nature of the cosmos.

To practice Ming (Body) Gong is to understand the subtlety of the human body, to master the natural laws of the continually transforming cosmos and to master your own life.

2. **<u>'Heaven And Human As One'</u>**

When the vibration of the human micro-cosmos and the Earth become resonant, a practitioner will experience spontaneous Qi Gong.

When the human micro-cosmos resonates with the rotation of the Earth, practitioners will experience the Mao-You cycle. The Qi of the human organs will flow and exchange Yin and Yang regularly within a 24 hour cycle.

**Zi (Baby Yang)**
Kidney Qi (Yuan Qi) Rises

**You (Sunset)**
Cultivate Lung Qi

**Mao (Sunrise)**
Cultivate Liver Qi

**Wu (Baby Yin)**
Cultivate Heart Qi

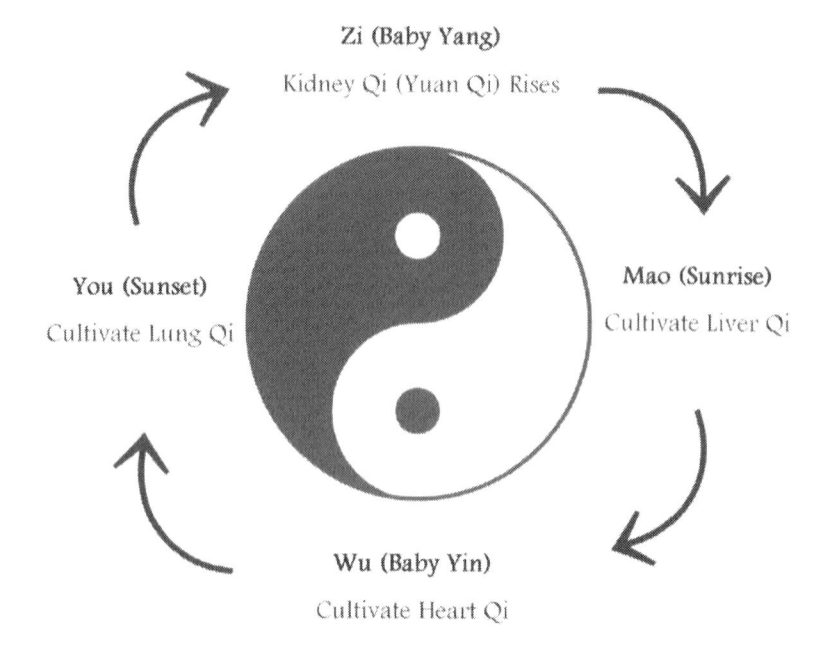

**Diagram of the Mao – You Cycle**

When the human micro-cosmos is resonant with the orbiting movements of the moon around the Earth, practitioners will experience the small cosmic orbit, i.e. the Qi of the five organs blending into oneness. The acquired Qi becomes full and the innate Qi becomes stronger. The Qi moves along the Ren and Du meridians. It passes the three gates, opens the top of the head and the third eye, goes to the lower three Dantian and continues to follow this cycle round and round continuously. Then inner and outer Qi will join together.

When the human micro-cosmos resonates with the rotation movement of the sun, practitioners will experience the big cosmic orbit. The inner Qi will move around the twelve meridian lines of the body constantly. The inner and outer Qi will resonate and become as one, bringing about all levels of 'heaven and human as one'.

## 3. <u>Motion and Stillness</u>

People, who are untrained, cannot control the movements of essence, Qi & spirit of their body through their mind. Their outer physical movement lacks the coordination with their inner movement. Therefore, the inner and outer cannot establish a synchronised 'motion and stillness' relationship.

When you are practicing moving Qi Gong, the outer physical movement takes the lead. The inner Qi will follow this lead and gradually rise, resulting in spontaneous Qi Gong, as well as spontaneous healing caused by Qi getting through to stagnant problem area. To begin with, the vigour and rhythm of the Qi is not very even, manifested by a lack of harmony between the internal and external, as well as the differing degrees of spontaneous movement. As the practice gets deeper and deeper, the inner Qi will more and more smoothly travel along the meridian system. The movement of moving Qigong likewise, will become more balanced, followed by a more symmetrical and regular paced routine. In the end, the practice will reach a state that when the body is moving, the inner Qi remains still – 'outer motion and inner stillness' - just like in Tai Ji.

When practicing stillness, the body appears motionless. However, the Qi is constantly moving through the meridians. This is called 'outer stillness and inner motion'.

When the inner Qi moves around the organs and meridian system on a regular basis and in accordance with macro-cosmic movements, inner and outer become synchronised and the practitioner experiences cosmic orbits. They will gradually enter a state of stillness. When Qi is in extreme stillness, the spirit will begin to awaken.

When the intellectual mind quiets down, the original spirit is unveiled. The original spirit is categorised into Yin spirit and Yang spirit. The Yin spirit will arise first and come irregularly at the beginning. After the continuous practice and adjustment, the Yin spirit will come regularly, allowing you to see your own heart, bone structure, blood vessels, meridian system, in short, the total view of your internal body. When the Yin spirit is complete in a still and quiet state, Yang spirit will eventually arise. It will be like a lovely and lively baby thrust out the top of the head and totally uncontrollable at first. Only through continuous and tenacious practicing, this tricky baby will finally be mastered.

Balancing and synchronising motion and stillness is the key to upgrading to higher dimensions by mastering the systematic rules and different levels of cultivation.

## 4. <u>Going Counter To Established Human Order Creates Immortals</u>

*"顺为人，逆为仙，只在其中颠倒颠"*

*"To follow human order, is to act like an ordinary mortal, to go counter to this, is to act like an immortal."* - Daoist Chinese Proverb

Practitioners who can practice universal truth and follow the laws of nature will be able to master their own fate. The human micro-cosmos is constituted by the physical body and the macro-cosmos is everything outside of the human body. For ordinary people will think the micro-cosmos of their body is all that they are, people who practice the true Dao only treat the body's micro-cosmos as a foundation.

Using the human micro-cosmos, the people who practice true Dao will refine their essence, manoeuvre their Qi and purify their spirit. They will change the shape and quality of their body into the shape and quality of the foetus.

The macro-cosmos provides the law of nature that people who practice the true Dao will follow. On the one hand, they are inactive, i.e. surrendering totally to the macro-cosmos and merging with it. Nevertheless, they are capable of acting on anything, as a result of their complete resonance with the Dao, the macro-cosmos.

| **Ordinary people** | **People who practice true Dao** |
|---|---|
| Eat a normal diet | Take in the essence and Qi of the cosmos |
| When asleep, use dreams to nourish the spirit | Sleep without dreams, but allow the original spirit to become active |
| Males discharge sperm, females discharged menstrual period | Male sperm does not leak, females stop menstrual discharge |
| Female Yin and male Yang join together as husband and wife | Find Yin and Yang within oneself and produce the foetus Dan as a result |
| Become worn out before aging | Return to youth after aging |
| Time is linear from beginning to end | Time is a two way traffic system that one can move back and forth freely within |

## Golden Dan Practice Program 1

| | | | | |
|---|---|---|---|---|
| Building Foundation | Cultivating Spirit | Stay Centered | Quiet the Mind (Relax the body) | |
| | | | Stop Thinking | |
| | | | Enter Quietness | |
| | | Mind | Turn the Gaze Inward | |
| | | | Stop Observing | |
| | | | Remain in Focus (Dantian) | |
| | | | Intention (yellow lady true earth 黃婆真土) | |
| | Cultivating Qi | Qi | Pre-Heavenly Qi | |
| | | | Post-Heavenly Qi | |
| | | Breathing | Normal Breathing | |
| | | | Reverse Breathing | |
| | | Adjusted Breathing | Foetus Breathing (internal) | |
| | | | Feet Breathing | |
| | | Energetic (Qi) State | Heavenly Gates: Front/Back, Ren/Du, 8 extras | |
| | | | Energy States: Gentle Fire, Strong fire, Bathing | |
| | Cultivating Shen and Essence (Jing) | Baby Yang Time | General Baby Yang | |
| | | | Live Baby Yang | |
| | | Qi Flow | Yang Fire (Ascending) | |
| | | | Yin Essence (Descending), Returning the Essence to Nourish the Brain | Flow an Reverse Flow |
| | | | | Set up the Flow (舐吸撮閉) |
| | | | | Shen and Qi Flow together |
| | | | Two Qi Emerging | |
| | Picking Up Kan (Water) and Filling Up Li (Fire) | | | |

## *Golden Dan Practice Program 2*

| | | | | |
|---|---|---|---|---|
| Cultivating Golden Alchemy (Immortal Technique) | Hundred Days | Medicine | Internal Medicine | Big medicine, Alchemy (Dan) |
| | | | External Medicine | |
| | | Birth of the Medicine: Moves from dark to light | | |
| | | Pick Up Medicine: Contract Anus, Look Up | | |
| | | Quantity of Medicine: Half Gold, Half Water | | |
| | | Cauldron | Upper Cauldron: Upper Dantian (泥丸), External Medicine (Use for Heavenly Circuit) | |
| | | | Lower Cauldron: Middle Dantian (黄庭), Small Cauldron, (Use for Internal Medicine) | |
| | | Furnace: Lower Dan Tian | | |
| | | Energetic State | Flow and Reverse Flow | |
| | | | Bathing | |
| | | | Small Cosmic Orbit | |
| | | Pick Up: identify, clean away all dirt, new or old, distinguish between gold and water and calculate the quantity | | |
| | | Seal: Pass through middle cauldron, Store in Lower Furnace, send to earth cauldron and seal | | |
| | | Cultivate: small cosmic orbit (300 breathes, 1500 days), merging | | |
| | | Stop: when the essence and spirit merge then stop the fire and move up to the middle Dantian | | |
| | | Alchemy (Dan) | Golden Alchemy (Divine Baby) | |
| | | | Small Medicine, Big Medicine | |
| | | Signal | | |
| | Ten Months (Transfer Qi into Spirit) | Merging internal and external medicine (seven days) | | |
| | | Big cosmic orbit rotating | | |
| | | Protection | | |
| | | Alchemical Formation (Big Alchemy, Original Spirit forms into an image) | | |
| | | Signs of formation (Six types of vibration, heavenly flowers drop, white snow flying) | | |
| | | Six miracle ESP's develop fully | | |
| | Nine Years (Cultivate Spirit, Return to the void) | Nourishing opening heavenly gate (top of head) | | |
| | | Protection from the devil | | |
| | | Out of body | | |
| | | Spirit travel | | |
| | | Return to the void | | |

# Glossary of Daoist Internal Alchemy

## Three Flowers On The Top Of The Head

The innate original essence, original Qi, and original spirit all concentrate in the Dantian and form a golden Dan. After going through internal alchemy processes of cultivating the essence into Qi, cultivating Qi into spirit and cultivating spirit to return to emptiness, the Yang spirit will come out of the top of the head.

## Five Qi Stays With The Original Self

- Body stillness - essence becomes strong so that water stays with the original self.
- Heart stillness - Qi becomes strong so that fire stays with the original self.
- The true spirit becomes quiet, the soul retreats so that wood stays with the original self.
- Illusory emotions are left behind, the soul lays down so that metal stays with the original self.
- The four directions of the spirit are in peace and the mind is still so that earth stays with the original self.

These mean the Qi of the five organs will all assemble at the Dantian and produce the golden Dan.

## Inner Vision and Inner Listening

Listen to the human heart – your own heartbeat.

Listen to the Dao's heart – the vibration of the Earth.

Listen to heaven's heart – the vibration of the cosmos.

Listening to the heart – when the heart is still that means the mind is still. This demonstrates that the five elements are centred and the internal point is very stable.

## Six Types Of Miracles (Extra-Sensory Perceptions)

The pure Yang spirit gives birth to wisdom. When the Dao foetus is formed, the foetus Qi will spontaneously appear before your eyes. This is the light of the true wisdom.

- Non-leakage miracle: The non-leakage of Qi is achieved after the cultivation of essence. The other five miracles can only be obtained after this first one is obtained
- Heavenly eye miracle: The light of the true wisdom allows you to see things happening in heaven.
- Heavenly ear miracle: The ability to hear the language of the cosmos.
- Fortune telling miracle: The ability to know previous life karma.
- Mind reading miracle: The ability to know what is going to happen in the future.
- Spiritual mirror miracle: The ability to transform negative energy and return it to original spirit.

# Part Three

# Chapter Seven
# Modern Internal Alchemy – Wakening People through Intensive Practices

When people open up a traditional internal alchemy book, they will first learn about weird things on subjects as diverse as mercury, spiritual living, young women, yellow old ladies, ox and deer carts, river carts, and so on. Readers generally don't know what the authors are talking about. Later on, they will read about concepts such as the dark entrance and the secret hidden cave, which will make them even more puzzled. To begin with readers may think that our ancestors were crazy!

The concepts that can be accepted by most are perhaps 'Essence, Qi, and Spirit'.

To use plain language, internal alchemy is about using our human body as an alchemical furnace, and treating each body cavity (tian) as a round cauldron; the abdominal, chest and brain cavities. The centre of each body cavity is the focal point where the energy is built up from low to high. Firstly, the common method of building essence are the following - through meditation to maintain inward peace, contracting the anus, slightly contracting the abdomen, breathing from the abdomen, collecting, retaining and accumulating energy.

The second step is turning this essence into Qi. This is achieved through taking care of and maintaining the body and sending the

Qi from each cavity's energy centre to the entire body, flowing through all the meridians points in the process and consequently letting the Qi flow smoothly through the entire meridian system.

The third step is to turn Qi into spirit. Through experiencing Qi communication and exchange with others, with plants and/or animals, and with invisible energies, the practitioner will come to realise that he or she and everything in the cosmos is inseparable. They will develop a kind of all-encompassing love including love of oneself, of others and of everything in existence. The practitioner will reach a state of internal harmony and peace. This is called Qi being transformed into spirit.

After these processes there are two final stages that can be described as 'returning spirit to emptiness' and 'practicing emptiness to be in accordance with the Dao.' When you're developing your spirit, your spirit will start to communicate and exchange with other spirits at a spiritual level. You will automatically take on larger issues, for example social responsibility, environmental protection or political participation for the public good and engage in altruistic and humane activities. The regular practice of body, mind, and spirit together will allow you to be connected to the wisdom of the cosmos and reach a state of complete perfection, i.e. the state of heaven and human as one. This is the process of returning spirit to emptiness and practicing emptiness to be in accordance with the Dao.

**To recap then, internal alchemy is, in a nutshell, about how to "practice essence and transform it to Qi, practice Qi and to transform it to spirit, practice spirit and to return to emptiness and practice emptiness to be in accordance with the Dao".**

To be in accordance with the Dao is achieved when you are able to tune into all the frequencies of vibration in the cosmos up to and including the eighth dimensional level. In this state, you will attain a complete freedom and perfection, capable of transforming and travelling through time and space. How can we enter this kind of field and get this kind of energy? You start by making the wish, accumulating the Qi, meditating to reach internal tranquillity and committing yourself to serious spiritual practices. In some schools of alchemy making the wish and practicing with strict discipline are essential steps of the full course. In fact, all the steps mentioned will have an influence on the Qi and the light energy fields. These fields change 24 hours a day over the course of our entire life. Therefore, we could say that our whole life is a training ground contained within a large alchemical furnace.

Regardless of whether you are aware of it or not, you cannot escape the alchemical furnace of the Earth and the cosmos, no more so than you can escape your own body's furnace. However, it is only when you are consciously making a wish to follow the steps of internal alchemy i.e. to be discreet about your practice, to accumulate Qi, meditate to reach tranquillity and commit to spiritual practices, are you then able to become a golden immortal. If you fail to do so, you are then likely to remain, on some level, wasteful and impure.

If your Qi is in reasonable shape, you may be fortunate enough to be thrown into the furnace again. However, if your Qi is bad, you will likely be completely removed with no more chances. At this juncture in time, every human being is being given the opportunity to evolve like never before and thus to be transformed.

Therefore, we say that internal alchemy is not an escape from reality, rather it is a system of different training and practice methods for living in the now - the only true reality there is. First, you must understand that your own body is a temple. The body is a system which has different Qi energy fields. It has potentials that can be developed, either from the top down or from the bottom up. Not only do you not need to rely on any external temple to practice, you can evolve into a state where your body and mind do not rely on the energy field of Earth at all, but instead the energy field of the cosmos.

The most common spiritual practices in everyday life are as follows:

Firstly, you have to be self-aware about your spiritual practices. You must understand that every thought and emotion will influence a change in your body's Qi field. This requires that you train in developing a steady state of consciousness which is peaceful, pure, ego-less, caring and loving. It helps if you are engaged in activities that benefit others or the public as a whole. When you are giving and making others happy, you will become happy within yourself, and the feeling of happiness will in turn cultivate a peaceful mind.

Taking actions to defend justice, helping the needy and the under privileged, and devoting yourself to selfless deeds will reinforce a positive Qi field and increase your purity and light.

In short, when a person is not running around only to meet his or her own selfish wants and needs, and when he or she is ready to open his or her heart, this is the key moment to open and enter into this high energy field.

In other words, when you are beyond self-interests, you are likely to be just, transparent and able to stay centred. To be just is also a way to keep the dirty, dark and heavy Qi energy out of one's energy field, i.e. when you are upholding justice you are pushing the impure Qi away from you. To disassociate from bad influences, to say no to greed, corruption and so on will help you maintain the purity of your Qi field.

In order to do all of these things, you have to live fearlessly in your social life. You have to dare to lose, to appear crazy and to reject the beliefs and habits that are suffocating the flow of your positive Qi. In the internal alchemy tradition unconventional, opposite and paradoxical thinking were encouraged. For example, if you want a long life, you must not be afraid of death; if you want to enter the light, you must be able to stay in darkness; if you want high energy, you must conserve energy in every moment and prevent your essence leaking. Normally, very outgoing and socially eloquent people are considered to be smart and popular whereas practitioners of internal alchemy actually need to be fairly unremarkable. **There is a saying in internal alchemy: "the majority of people follow conventional ways, the immortal knows to do the opposite." Internal alchemy emphasises the importance of having the courage to challenge the existing order.**

Some years ago an English musician came to my clinic to seek treatment for her breast cancer. We discussed her potential treatment plan in which I strongly suggested that she stop all her work, rest and relax, and concentrate on the treatment. She said that she had already arranged some future engagements. I asked her the question 'to be or not to be?' I told her that the breast cancer was sending her a strong warning that she had to change. A sensible person would stop and think about this situation when it is apparent that their way of living and thinking had led to this outcome. She immediately understood what I was expressing and agreed to cancel all her work schedule and appointments. She then began to practice Qi Gong and received regular acupuncture treatments. At the same time, the hospital urged her to undertake radiotherapy and chemotherapy treatment. She came to me and asked me for advice as to what she should do. I said to her that she had to follow her heart. She said she was torn between the two, believing on the one hand in self-healing through Qi Gong, but on the other hand, she was afraid that she would encounter problems if she did not follow the hospital's recommendation. Therefore, we started the treatment of 'combined Chinese and Western medicine'. Every time, after a large dosage of radiotherapy and chemotherapy, she would immediately come to my clinic to receive acupuncture which helped in the relief of the painful reactions to nausea and vomiting. She also continued to faithfully practice Qi Gong. As a result, the old grey hair that was falling out from the chemotherapy grew back as dark hair and even her wrinkles began to disappear. She was transforming into a different kind of beauty.

In internal alchemy meditation and Qi Gong classes, she often shared her experiences of inner light. At the beginning there were small sparkles. Later, the small sparkling light became light clouds. Eventually, one day she saw, with her eyes closed, that the room was full of golden light. She opened her eyes to check what was going on and found that the sky outside was actually completely cloudy. Her health condition improved gradually and she even started to go back to work. Moreover, she and her husband adopted a very lovely smart young boy.

This female musician was a very quiet and introverted person. In every Qi Gong class, I saw that her eyes were shining. She told me that her heart was full of joy and peace. Her only burden was the hospital trips. Every time she went to hospital, she felt helpless as she was considered to be 'fatally ill'. She could sense a dark Qi energy in the hospital which frightened her and made her feel helpless. But every time she came to do Qi Gong and for an acupuncture treatment, she would feel full of hope and relief.

Two years passed and she was doing very well. I moved from Newcastle to a small town near Oxford. As a result, my Qi Gong teaching in the Northeast of England stopped. Half a year later I received a call from her and she said she was not able to walk any more. I was very surprised. She told me the whole story - she had been to the hospital to have her cancer check-up but after one week she had not heard back from the hospital. She dared not ask and so just waited and waited. She was worrying too much and, consequently, was not able to meditate very well. Nor could she sleep which caused discomfort throughout her whole body. Her husband became concerned and took her to see a psychiatrist. The psychiatrist suggested that she take up some form of physical exercise, such as swimming. So she dragged her miserable body and bad mood to the pool and began to swim. However, because her Yang Qi was so weak she caught a cold. From there, her legs became numb, which limited her mobility and led her to become even more depressed. Two weeks had now passed and one of her friends persuaded her to call the hospital and ask for the result. So she finally called. The nurse who answered the phone said in a very light hearted way: "The result is clear. You are fine. It came out a long time ago but we must have forgotten to notify you. Sorry about that."

By this time however, she had almost become paralysed and was unable to get out of bed. Soon she lost control of her bowel movements. She tragically died a few months later. Put simply, the thing that killed her and totally depleted her very good (high and light) Qi energy field was nothing more than fear.

The process of practicing Dan is the process of enduring various pains and suffering that stem from society, family, or even the self. People like to blame the failure of achieving Dan on external influences. For instance, in the story of this musician, many people's first reaction might be to blame the nurse. Most people would not consider that the nurse might have been merely unconsciously acting on behalf of the heavens to train this musician to overcome her fear.

Practicing internal alchemy is not what people imagine whereby Daoist practitioners live comfortably in beautiful natural surroundings, deep in the mountains or woods with nothing to disturb them. Practicing Dan's high energy vibration means that you have to have the courage to surrender, to defy convention, even at the most difficult and hopeless of times. To be able to do this, you need to develop your state of mind - your consciousness

- through meditation, and go beyond ego, attachment and doubt, fear, guilt, and laziness. When you experience almost unbearable suffering, this is the indication that purification is taking place. Your impurities are melting away from you so that the bright Dan within can be revealed. Many people give up at this most critical moment because they cannot endure the discomfort. When the fire starts, they effectively stop the fuel, or stop the process. The result will be a defective product that will eventually have to go back to the furnace again. Only this next time it will take even longer and require enduring even greater pain in order to reach Dan.

Our society is a big alchemical furnace. We often see people who are working very hard taking care of their family and others. Being so busy they aren't able to spend any time just to be quiet. Consequently they can develop many unresolved issues that tangle their heart and are akin to being on an unconscious non-stop train that is ultimately going nowhere. By the age of forty or fifty, with their children becoming independent adults, they think that they can be more relaxed and, at last, have more time for themselves. However, many health problems can start to surface at this point. It can seem that life is playing a trick on them. Actually though, these are typically necessary warnings in the alchemical process. If the messages that these life events signify are not correctly interpreted and understood, then ill health and/or misfortune will prevail.

When these warnings appear in the form of bad luck occurring in your own life, you must stop and think quietly for a moment. You must wait for the voice of your heart to make itself known, and then start to take action. The best way will be to help oneself, to heal oneself, and thus self-improve. Relying on the living vitality contained within our own inner being we are then able to open up the light. We have to mobilise the strength that is naturally stored in our bodies. Through spiritual practice, we release our existing potentials. The truth then reveals itself to us eventually.

We can train ourselves to hear the voices of the higher order immortals that can be heard only if our egos do not interfere. When you develop your wisdom through connecting with the great wisdom of the macro-cosmos, you will no longer be entangled by concerns of personal gain and loss. During this period, you should learn to use pain as a signal to guide you in overcoming existing problems, such as ego and attachment. For instance, all the fatigue and bodily pains you experience are telling you what parts of you are still restless and causing leakage of Dan, Qi and light. Fear can be one of the most common reasons of Qi energy leakage. Other common causes are addictions to sensual pleasure, drug dependency, alcohol, fame, wealth etc. Sometimes, you might be excited by a big house or simply a beautiful piece of silk or maybe you want a person to love you so badly that you feel you're going crazy. You become the victim of all these low energy level desires and end up walking on a tightrope path of gradual 'suicide'.

Another terrible cause of Dan leakage is guilt. When people suffer from a sense of guilt, they either develop anger or aggression toward themselves, or feel hopeless and heavily burdened. How can you imagine a person to truly love others and be happy if they do not like themselves? Let alone expect them to be able to lift the level of their own energy field. One more significant cause of Dan leakage is laziness. When gold first comes out of the earth, it looks pretty much like soil. Therefore, without smelting, the gold can never be transformed.

In the ancient books of Chinese internal alchemy, Dan is often referred to as medicine. Let us look at the course of events in the smelting of Dan, so as to help us appreciate the importance of the heart and this medicine.

To practice, we should know the methods and the procedures. First, we must understand that the body is a micro-cosmos. We must give enough attention to the body which is the 'material' foundation in the practice of Dan. For instance, we have to set up the cauldron and prepare its condition. Specifically, our body posture must be correct. Our spine must be straight and our body must be firm, stable and solid like a pyramid. The best posture for meditation is sitting in the lotus posture. Also, to prepare your body, you should wash and clean your body using hot water to open up the bottom meridian.

Secondly, it is extremely important to purify your heart, to eliminate impure thoughts so that one can be at peace. All desires, big or small, can cause the medicine (meaning the origin of the essence, Qi and spirit), to leave the alchemical cauldron. When people have many thoughts in their mind, their attention goes outward. Significant amounts of essence, Qi and spirit will leave the Dan field. So, the first lesson in practice is to train the focus of your consciousness and to keep to this focus. Developing and keeping this focus is fundamental to the process of collecting one's essence, Qi and spirit. When you practice to a level where you can feel the movement of the original essence, Qi and spirit inside of your body, you will be able to consciously collect all of them and restore them back to your Dan field.

We say that to purify your heart is a prerequisite in the lifelong practice of internal alchemy. If your heart is closed, you will have fear which will hurt and darken your kidney. This fear will lead to defensive concepts and behaviours, which in turn will cause conflict. All these will create large quantities of bodily toxins that will damage the physical body and speed up the aging process. Only when we can overcome our fear and scepticism (i.e. scepticism of the existence of high energy vibration fields and the miracles of these energy fields), will our heart be able to release its energy. At that point, other minor problems will more easily resolve as well.

When faced with a complicated situation, we seek the truth of simplicity. The ultimate truth is always the simplest. We need to learn to be concise, and to talk less. Even when we're dealing with a large influx of information, we should aim to be humble and discreet. Such an approach will help us to maintain our Qi and keep our heart quiet. Retaining a stable Qi field will enable us to continue to do well at everything.

We are in the midst of emotional, material, belief and information fields. Vibrations of fear and anxiety are stronger than ever before which creates additional challenges to people who want to practice internal alchemy. Whether or not we will be able to prevail over such heavy and impure surroundings, to put aside a plethora of seductions, to firmly keep our inner peace, and to collect the golden Dan back to our Dantian remains to be seen. It sounds simple, but it is hugely challenging, especially for the training of the mind to live in a moment by moment manner. It is a test to see if we are able to completely surrender and keep to simplicity within the complexity and constant demands of modern living.

The third important step is called "growing the medicine, collecting the medicine and covering the cauldron". When we speak of 'growing the medicine' it means the appearance of light. Internal alchemy books often use the phrase "the image of the growing medicine", which describes the experience when Qi and light energy appears. You will feel a very warm sensation coming from the lower Dantian (below your navel) that will fill up your whole body and make you feel extremely relaxed and blissful.

The Qi will come up from the kidneys to the heart and then return to the kidneys. Representing the exchange of Yin and Yang, the Qi will move back and forth between the kidneys and heart. It is what the ancient books called water and fire's mutual nurturing. This practice will lead to a warm sensation in the hands and feet and the complete Qi flow of the 'small cosmic orbit'. At this stage, one should keep their attention and consciousness inward and not allow the intrusion of rational and intellectual thinking.

Eyes should stay closed to remain in darkness. In the macrocosmos 95% of particles are comprised of dark matter and dark energy therefore you must dare to stay in the dark so that you may then sense the light. Internal alchemy needs to go through the process of darkness, to lightness, to white light and lastly golden light. This is called the principle of believing the white while staying in the dark. The light will appear from sparkles and gradually accumulate. You will overcome fear by constantly staying in a state of peace and quietude. Sometimes it can be more effective to attend a short-term retreat where the power of a collective Qi field can help each individual student obtain bigger light spots and lessen impurity, and thus approach Dan more quickly.

This period is like that of the monkey-king Sun Wu Kong's experience inside the alchemical furnace. His eyes could not see anything and he was suffocating and suffering from the deadly heat. He was born as a relentlessly rebellious fighter and carefree spirit, but ended up being tortured in the dark furnace where he could neither escape nor die. This is the exact situation facing human beings at the moment. We are experiencing the painful trial of alchemy.

Rebecca is a student who attended my Qi Gong classes all over the world for more than ten years. When she first came she had a big tumour, as big as a watermelon, inside her abdomen. She faithfully practiced the Mao-You cosmic orbit Qi Gong and in so doing gradually became more and more relaxed. As she became more relaxed, repressed emotions started to burst forth like volcanic eruptions. At first, she was somewhat scared. During Qi Gong practice, I taught the principles of surrender, asking them to follow the flow of their Qi. When she followed this principle, she began to cry and scream which frightened her. She wanted, on several occasions, to stop coming to my classes. However, through the processes of emotional release and cleansing, she began to become less attached to her ego. She effectively came out of a cage of self-victimisation where she blamed everybody, including her mother and work colleagues. She, therefore, became even more relaxed and let the Qi flow naturally which often resulted in self-beating and loud screaming or wailing. Many classmates became very annoyed by her spontaneous Qi Gong and thought she had serious mental problems. But she did not let this concern her. Eventually, she became so relaxed that she was able to be quiet. In her day to day life she changed into a new person. She became very generous and helpful to friends and colleagues. Without any surgery, her tumour mysteriously disappeared. In internal alchemy though, there was nothing mysterious about it. It was the Dan medicine that had healed her.

I often meet people who ask me something along the lines of "Why do you say it is necessary to go through such hard training that 'burns people up'? Didn't Lao Zi say in the *Dao De Jing* that we should aim for a state of deep relaxation? Shouldn't practicing Qi Gong make us feel good and allow things to take their natural course instead of pushing for things to happen?" Many people use this kind of rationale to justify their laziness. Indeed, Lao Zi did describe a very relaxed state as being "seemingly in a dream, seemingly in reality". He also followed this by saying that there is 'essence (Jing, 精)' and 'Xin (信)' in this state. Jing here means very fine and delicate whereas Xin means messages or information, i.e. the messages we receive from above. These messages can only be received when we are in a very still and peaceful state whereby we are so relaxed that it feels like we are in a dream – actually though we are very alert and conscious. If there are many noisy thoughts interfering with the channel of vibration, or the meridian points are all blocked, we will not be able to receive the very fine and delicate signals from heaven. This need not be hard to understand.

If you throw a stone in a very still lake, you will clearly see the ripples made by the stone. If you throw this same stone in a stormy ocean, you will not see any effect. It is also like using a radio to receive certain frequency channels. Your body has to be sensitive enough to pick up the right frequency, and this sensitivity is related to your purity and state of emptiness and the vibration of your energy field. When you are in an absolute still and empty state, you will be able to receive any kind of frequencies in the cosmos. The more still and quiet you are, the easier it is to tune into the cosmos. You can then easily access the great wisdom of the cosmos.

Over ten years ago now, I guided a group to tour some of China's famous mountains and rivers to practice Qi Gong. We stayed at the famous Daoist Mountains of Lao Shan for seven days. During this time, we spent two days practicing Qi Gong on a big rock called Hun Yuan. According to legend, Lao Zi had practiced on that very rock. After the first day's practice, one student, who was already very sensitive, came to me and asked: "What do the words 'Lao Shan Zhen Dao' mean?" She did not know any Chinese at all but was repeating the sound of this phrase that she had heard. I was surprised and replied: "Where did you hear this?" She said that when she was meditating on the rock, she saw a Daoist fly across the sky toward her and say to her "Lao Shan Zhen Dao" (translated to English it means: Lao Mountain's true Daoism). Then the Daoist, who was now standing in front of her, became a small baby and sat beside her. Later, the baby sat facing her for a while and then melted into the rock and disappeared. After her encounter with this Daoist, she began to sense other people's consciousness and Qi fields. She told me that she liked China very much and that she had these kinds of experiences more easily in China than in London, where she was from. She could feel herself getting lighter and more transparent. She was, of course, able to have these experiences because she had entered a still and quiet state and because of her innate acuity in picking up these higher vibrational frequencies. However, in the busy and noisy larger cities and when overwhelmed by daily worries and thoughts, her ability to access these faculties lessened.

If our mind and consciousness are in a turbulent state, our meridian system will become blocked. We need a total repair and a thorough cleaning in order to get rid of impurities. Before then, it will not be possible to practice Dao. Hedonists and escapists are led astray by very selfish motives which represent very low energy fields. Unless you set in motion the process of cleansing these low energies you will not then be in a position to experience the great wisdom of the cosmos.

# Chapter Eight
# Couples Practice, Solitary Practice, Early Practice

## Couples Practice

Once while chatting with a friend we started talking about an old man. Aged 80 he had married a young wife and had in fact married over 19 times. This friend said "It seems that this old guy practices 'Xing' (性) a lot (the Chinese character for which means human nature as well as sexuality). The Daoists were right when they said that to practice Xing (性) and Ming (命, life, fate, fortune) at the same time, one needs to have had good sex first, and then he can enjoy a good life." I was amazed how this Daoist principle could be twisted in such an absurd way.

I immediately said "In the Daoist's meaning of practicing Xing (性) and Ming (命) at the same time, the Xing (性) does not mean human or other animal sexuality but, rather, it means the spiritual nature of human beings. The merger of Xing (性) and Ming (命) practices together means that the soul (性) and the body (命) will be practiced together." In an earlier chapter, we mentioned that the Xing (性) practice of Daoists includes the following aspects: immortal spirit, soul, determination, will (志), tranquillity, and light.

However, I think what my friend said brings to the surface some issues that need to be addressed:

1. Many people have heard about 'couples practice' or 'Yin and Yang practice' in Daoism (meaning when a man and woman practice together) and they often associate this practice with the Daoist term 'Xing (性) and Ming (命) practice together', which is the principle of practicing the merging of soul and body together. The methodology of man and woman practicing together is also widely mentioned on various websites. Indeed, many western internal alchemists choose not to talk about Daoist internal alchemy, because they are concerned that their message may get confused with couples practice concepts that are themselves so often associated with prurience.

2. For Daoists, couples practice is based on the deep understanding of human nature and, as such, is considered to be a secret practice method. It has very strict disciplines. If one wants to practice it, he or she has to learn to be discreet, maintain their energy and not to divulge the method. It is generally only taught to students who have reached a level that is beyond sexual desire, and not to those who are still having sexual desires.

3. Some people are motivated by economic interests. Taking advantage of westerners' curiosity in Daoist myths, they publish books or develop training programs to attract business. It is a shame that this secretive Eastern practice method has become popular in the West. But if we think a little more carefully then we will realise that the practice of being mindful in every moment and aspect of our lives will also naturally and inevitably encompass love making too. Internal alchemy, especially the practice of the immortal spirit, requires practice in every moment. Just as alchemists say: "Xing Gong (soul

and spiritual practice) should be practiced in every moment; Ming Gong (physical practice) however can be practiced at selected and/or the correct time intervals." This means that physical practice ideally needs to be carried out in accordance with changes in the natural environment (i.e. the seasons of the year and the times of each day) while the practice of Xing (性), the soul and immortal spirit, must be performed anytime, anywhere, more especially when you are using a lot of your life force energy. It is a huge challenge to keep your awareness, consciousness and the focus of your centre while in the midst of sensual activities. It is, however, an important part of internal alchemy.

The Yin and Yang (man and woman) couples practice was originally a secret practice method. It is a direct and swift method that goes through the central spine meridian and relies on the strong life energy released through the process of sexual intercourse. The excitement and vibration of sexual power can unblock the major points of the meridians allowing Qi to flow smoothly, so that Dan can then be obtained. It uses a bigger Qi vibration to control the body's life force energy, and uses the latter to its full extent.

During this process, the mind and soul must be pure and empty and, at the same time, the practitioner must acutely notice, observe and control every delicate change of Qi and light within their body. Sometimes, one can experience thunder and strong light which will help to open up the meridians. One can also experience the majestic feeling of body and soul merging into the infinite universe. This is a path that goes through the stages of desire and lust and, crucially, beyond, in order to elevate the practitioners' energy dimensions. They will go beyond the entanglement of desire and become lighter and brighter. It is through the exchange of Qi and energy vibration that a man and woman can help each other unblock their meridians and raise their frequency levels to reach a state of complete perfection and enlightenment. At the same time it can heal bodily stagnations and imbalances.

In the past, the Dan classics often talk about how a man would seek out a woman and would pick a woman according to their Qi quality. In fact, the female Dan practitioner also needs to find men of high Qi quality to practice Dan. In this sense, man and woman are completely equal.

'Couples practice' is quick to open meridian blockages compared to 'solitary practice'. It is completely different from ordinary sexual intercourse which can be seen more as a way of simply releasing physical tension. 'Couples practice' uses physical energy to raise light energy as opposed to the usual downward release of energy. When practiced well one will feel very clear-minded, energetic, lighter and glowing after practice, which is totally opposite to the after-effects of ordinary sexual intercourse of feeling fatigued and somewhat hollow.

Moreover, when you practice 'couples practice' very well, your sexual desire will actually decrease. You become more tuned into the spiritual Qi field and will become pickier about other people's energy levels and less particular about their appearances. You will feel more congenial to higher spiritual and lighter Qi fields and less attracted by low energy level activities. You will develop the ability to detect the characteristics of different frequency levels sent out by different bodies and souls.

## Solitary Practice

The word 'Qing' (清 clear, solitary) describes the nature of this school of spiritual practice. In Chinese, Qing is often associated with Xiu (修) practice. It is a practice method of uplifting energy fields which does not involve the physical energy exchange between a man and woman. In this kind of practice, one has to have a very clear grasp of one's own vibration field and the external vibration field. For people who are firmly rooted in the Daoist tradition, this method is considered far superior. It is a method to screen and optimise the large amount of external energy and information to a very minimum level when the practitioner enters the state of stillness and tranquillity. It especially disengages the practitioner from interpersonal emotional interferences. In this way one can maximise his or her connection with nature's five elements coming from the cosmos, Earth and plants and use their Qi to build up the practitioner's energy level.

The most common practice is to live an extremely regular lifestyle; for the body's Qi field to live in accordance with the changes of the natural Qi field in terms of its cycles, such as the movement of the sun (Yang) and the moon (Yin). It emphasises four times of day, where each time slot has a particular type of exchange between the energies of Yin and Yang. The first time slot is sunrise. This is when the practice is to watch the sun, to be outdoors and active and to practice Qi Gong, letting Yang Qi rise. The second time slot is midday and is when one should take a rest to help nourish the heart Yin. The third time slot is sunset, and is for collecting Yang Qi. And finally the fourth time slot is midnight when it is ideal for sitting meditation and connecting to the spirit Qi.

This kind of method is learning to tune one's body to the rhythm of the cosmos on a day by day, year by year basis. In this way, the foundation of alchemy is very solid. When the body is steady and solid, the mind will be calm and small interruptions will make no impact whatsoever to one's Qi field.

Solitary practice can be a practice for a whole life such as is practiced by many Daoist and Buddhists living in the remote and secluded areas of the world. They prefer living in solitude and keep far away from all worldly matters. However, solitary practice can also be a periodical or temporary practice, such as the practice of Bi Guan (闭关); a period of living in closed off isolation. Sometimes, when the practitioner has reached a certain level, where the Qi field is very open, the physical body becomes transparent. At this point one is ready for 'Zhong Ju' (冲举); a burst of light and separation of body and spirit. During this critical period the external influence of impure Qi can be very harmful. Therefore, it is very sensible to go into temporary solitary practice. Of course, if a person has reached a very high level of stillness, he or she is able to enter this high vibrational state anywhere and at any time without being influenced. That is a characteristic attribute that internal alchemy, Dan, can produce.

Using the analogy of the alchemical cauldron, 'couples practice' is to add fuel to your own bodily fire, and blowing in air so that the fire in the furnace will create greater heat. Therefore the Dan will be ready at a faster pace. In this case, the quality of the fuel must be good as bad quality fuel will have the opposite effect. That is to say, the partners of couples practice must have a good Qi level. The true internal alchemy practitioner will understand that it is better to take the slow route by solitary practice than the quicker couples practice if the quality of the fuel is poor, because the poor quality fuel will not only ruin the Dan, but also harm the practitioner. In addition, the heat and air must be controlled in a proper way, i.e. the movements, the breathing during the practice and especially the management of consciousness. Consciousness and will can be very powerful energies which can immediately trigger the heat of the fire. Therefore, it can be quite risky. It requires solid stillness and the right methodology.

The analogy of solitary practice in terms of alchemy is like a cauldron sitting at a warm and constant temperature. It has no significant ups and downs and therefore involves less risk. It is a gradual process to smelt the impurities. When there is a lack of fuel, one will get it from nature. The heat of the furnace is constantly adjusted to maintain a reliable and steady temperature. Just as a quiet lake with its mirror-like surface can exactly reflect nature without distortion, so it is with great clarity and purity in the heart and soul.

When solitary practice reaches a certain degree and stage, the furnace will be closed. The three Dantian will have accumulated enough warm heat which will begin to rise. The Yin and Yang exchange within one's own body will occur generating a large Qi and light field (See Chapter 6). This is when the practice of Dan - gathering the Dan and returning the Dan to golden Dan has been completed.

In today's terribly polluted environment no one can really live in the deep mountain temples as hermits did in ancient times. This kind of special clean and quiet place is unfortunately no longer attainable. In order to minimise the interference from outside, and speed up internal alchemy, the most important method is to learn how to keep the inner quietness in every moment. You must be very alert and aware, in order to keep the purity, clarity, stillness and quietness of your heart and consciousness, and keep the dirty Qi out of your energy field so that it will not contaminate your cauldron. You should never compromise with any suboptimal conditions, such as fear, emotional indulgence, lack of compassion, guilt, laziness, dependence on material and sensual gratification, etc.

The solitary practice is to learn how to live as a lotus; in the midst of dirt and mud yet not even be slightly contaminated. You are constantly in a still and silent state, when you are eating, sleeping, working or practicing Qi Gong. When you are eating, you experience your food, and observe how the food influences your Qi. Then you will understand why you should be a vegetarian. The change from eating meat to vegetables, to water, to light, corresponds to human evolution from the third and fourth dimensional level to the seventh and eighth level.

When famine comes, people with higher dimensional vibrations can survive by getting energy charged by the cosmos, i.e. the light.

Emotion is related to internal alchemy practices. You can observe your Qi under an anxious mood or a quiet mood. Certain sounds can influence the body's meridians and unblock the stagnant points. The house you are living in can also influence the Qi field changes of internal alchemy practice. Theories of Feng Shui (风水) assess how the human body's Qi field interacts with the Qi field of the environment and has been studied for more a thousand years. For example when you are asleep your Qi is quiet and Yang is withdrawing. Therefore the bedroom should not be too big. In our modern times people think that the bigger the bedroom, the more luxurious. In the ancient times, even the emperors, who could have built a bedroom as big as they wished, understood the bedroom had to be small so that it would be easier to recover the Qi. When Qi is well collected and kept, it will not leak Dan.

To practice alchemy when you are meditating is not very difficult. It is more difficult to practice Dan in normal life when you are engaged in each moment of life. To be able to practice in every present moment you will be a master. If you keep remembering Dan is a high frequency light, it will be easier for you to practice Dan in everyday actions, i.e. when you are doing things in accordance with the principles of the large cosmos, and universal truth, you will be staying in the high frequency field. You have to see through your ego and let it go, only then will you be able to connect your consciousness to cosmic consciousness and truth. That is when miracles will take place. The universal truth is love, love of self and of people, unconditionally. To focus on this is to stop conflict and cruelty towards yourself and others, and to constantly seek to self-purify and self-improve. It is to empty yourself when in the still and quiet state so that you can communicate with higher cosmic spirits and to attain the great wisdom from the cosmos. This wisdom is embedded in every moment of our lives and therefore is always there waiting to be obtained in any given moment.

No matter if it is couples practice or solitary practice, both schools of practice are a bottom up approach, i.e. they start practicing with your body and your way of living (e.g. your lifestyle and discipline of daily practice). This sets your micro-cosmos to be in tune with the macro-cosmos. It is to merge your every motion, sentiment and thought with the Earth and cosmos' Qi field.

Praying, mantras etc. are to practice in a top down approach. It is a method of communication between humans and the immortals or humans with heaven. Here I am speaking about when you have deep wishes, when the power of your will is pushed by the Qi and sends them out to the cosmos, you try to send the messages to the spirit or the cosmic consciousness. When the immortal spirit or cosmic consciousness receives your signals, they will respond. Sometimes, people notice the response, sometimes people do not. When people notice, they will see miracles happen in their lives or things begin to happen as they wished.

When we obtain the Dan light of the high vibration field, our consciousness will be linked directly to the macro-cosmos consciousness. When you are connected with the macro-cosmos you will not be troubled by mundane thoughts. Your behaviour will be in accordance with the principles and standards of alchemy.

The vibration of prayer and making wishes are related to a frequency of light. When the motivation is pure the wishes will likely be connected to the high frequency immortals and their consciousness.

The will of a sage is borne highly; it has very great power which allows them to travel freely in the universe, beyond the realm of time and space.

To live peacefully is the wish of ordinary people. It is also a state of being, but is of a lower level. This state is more vulnerable to being overpowered by larger and stronger energy fields. For instance, when the global environment is changing, brought about by natural and human catastrophes, an individual or small group's wishes for well-being can be very powerless.

Many people, who are busily consumed by their daily lives, will only turn to prayer to ask for heaven's help and to make wishes once a crisis has already occurred. But the truth is 'God helps the people who help themselves'. The better approach is to practice diligently before a crisis so that you will know what to do when disaster comes.

## **Early Practice**

Early practice is a traditional practice and teaching method. It chooses individuals who have very relevant roots and backgrounds (e.g. certain experiences in past lives) to start as soon as the children are born. These children's teachers could be their grandparents, or parents or other significant people. They will be trained physically and spiritually from the very beginning of their lives, from every detail of physical and psychological upbringing. People being trained early on need to be enlightened about what his or her special missions are and why he or she came to the Earth, and also how to lead other human beings to develop consciousness in accordance with Dao. They are the ones to hold the torch and lead the people in the darkness. They must learn to carry and pass on the wisdom, to express and disseminate wisdom using their words and their actions. Some of them need to live through very painful and difficult life experiences. Others may not need that since they have had their trials in other lives or other dimensional existences. In general, they are here to perform their duty, i.e. the tasks of helping human beings to open up their hearts, to lead them toward higher level dimensional beings and to be able to continue their journey in other spaces, i.e. to be transformed when the moment of transformation comes.

# Chapter Nine

# Internal Alchemy – The Effective 'Medicine' That Gives Human Beings New Hope

Human beings are a species that are inclined to spirituality. Of course, animals and plants have spirits too. Humans have an advantage though with their creative and initiative capacities. We have both egoic and self-examinination mechanisms. The two mechanisms are like Yin and Yang. If the ego is too big, and there is a lack of checking or balancing through self-reflection and examination, humans will expand their ego and physical territory irrationally. Their intelligence and creativity will be misused destroying each other and causing the destruction of the environment. These activities are irrational because they will inevitably lead to the eventual self-destruction of the human race. However, the blinded unchecked ego will not be able to see the consequences of its behaviour. But if human beings can use their self-examining capability to exercise self-control, they will be able to continue on their course of evolution.

Introspection (self-examination) is a very important aspect of internal alchemy. In fact, it is the first step in practice. If everybody were to constantly supervise each of their thoughts and actions and make sure they are in accordance with Dao, the civilisation of Earth would be very advanced.

The practice of internal alchemy is seeking the proof of truth inside the mind and soul and it can only be realised by living the truth in action. Therefore, it is the most direct pathway for human beings to pursue progression and a bright future.

The purpose of internal alchemy is to set human beings free from limitations and constraints, so that they can experience the multi-dimensional nature of the cosmos through following body, mind and soul practices. It is the living proof and model of what is possible when human beings evolve to the higher states. In history, there have already been many successful cases to prove this. During the course of Earth's drastic changes in the future, there will be more people who can develop these kinds of experiences so that we can eventually live harmoniously with other cosmic civilisations.

Everybody has to face their own health problems and care about their own body's condition to varying degrees. However, the relationship between the body and soul is like the relationship between a car and its driver. If you only take care of your body, but not your soul, it is like a good car without a sensible driver. This driver can be drunk or insane which can lead to an accident destroying both the driver and the car. If the car is getting old, but the driver is very experienced and with a very good mentality and attitude, the car can still last a long time. And if the driver is in good shape, he or she can afford to move to a better or brand new car.

To care more about the car than the driver is a common human trait nowadays. Many people spend lots of money and time to maintain their health or body, but neglect the care of their soul and spirituality. It is not unlike letting your driver starve whilst using all the resources to wax, polish and beautify the appearance of the car; when the driver starts to drive, something is bound to then go wrong.

The practice of internal alchemy tries to take care of the driver, as well as the car. It is a good method to care for both the soul and the body at the same time through practice.

As we go deeper through the course of internal alchemy practice, we human beings will evolve into highly qualified pilots so that we can drive our bodies as spaceships to travel freely throughout the cosmos.

It is said that the practice of internal alchemy is the only way to save our human race, both individually and collectively. Relying only on external forces to survive will be futile.

Future disasters are also mechanisms for selection. The people who have enough light and Qi will be able to sustain and survive the trials; the ones who do not have enough light and Qi will perish. If you become one with the cosmic consciousness or Dao, you will live together with Dao. If you are not with Dao, i.e. living against nature, you will be discarded and returned to basic particles to start all over again.

The Dao is nature and is cultivation. The principle of Dao is to follow nature. The person who cultivates based on the principles of nature will become immortal. All true spiritual practices on this earth are in line with the universal laws of nature.

The energy level of human souls is judged by their ability to love and their alignment with Dao. We often say 'go with the flow'. This 'flow' is the nature of the big cosmos. Disasters are also natural processes. If people disobey nature, they will be warned and punished. Worldly disasters are like the spontaneous Qi Gong of the Earth. It has its own mechanism for readjusting. It's as if the information system of Earth is sending out signals. The working mechanism is not unlike our own body. When the problem is minor, the signals will be minor; when the problem is big, the signals will be big. We human beings are like the cells of the Earth. The rivers on Earth are like the body fluid and blood system of our bodies. The pollution in these rivers is like the illnesses in our blood systems that cause the blockages in blood vessels. The water problem on Earth is like the blood and body fluid systems of the human body having problems. It will impact the whole body. The hardening of the soil and the growing deserts are akin to the stiffness of our muscles, and are caused by a lack of water.

In Chinese medicine, blood and liver are related to the nervous system and the soul and mind. If you want your blood to be healthy and the circulation to be smooth, you need to cultivate your soul and spirit. In other words, you need to practice spirituality. When your mind and soul have problems, you are effectively 'insane' and, consequently, your behaviour will be destructive to all including yourself.

The reason human beings should practice internal alchemy also touches a very sensitive issue; why have we come to this world in the first place? What are we here for? What is the meaning of our lives? The answer is clear; we are here to practice Dao, to create and align with the energy field that is at one with the heavens. This is the sole reason why we come here to live, to learn, to experience various physical and psychological sensations. It is all part of the training and practice. We learn not to be trapped by the low energy field of physical and material gratification. We learn how to evolve from low to high by experiencing light. When we talk about spiritual practice, the aspect people are most afraid of is what they call being infatuated and misled (by demons). Ironically, what they don't realise is the fact that believing only in the visible, physical and material world as the sole truth and reality *is* the most serious infatuation and delusion of our time. And the fear of infatuation itself can be a demon, because 'fear' is a demon itself.

Human beings must overcome the fear in order to join the oneness of the Dao, and keep out the demons. Then we will be elevated. The fear is in fact the fear of losing what we have now. It is fear of change. But this is against Dao and nature, because change is an inevitable and timeless truth.

Human beings can only be merged with nature if we can rise above our fear and maintain the same calmness and alertness to follow the flow of changing nature. This nature includes your contract with the larger cosmic consciousness. You have agreed to come here to contribute and take responsibility to accomplish certain deeds. The cosmos will arrange everything based on this agreement. However, if you don't do what you agreed to do, the consequence is that you will have affected the agreements of others around you as well as the unfoldment of the cosmic plan. Therefore, we say following the flow of nature also means to cultivate a humble and trustworthy attitude toward the macro-cosmos.

As cosmic time and space are beyond our very limited imagination, we cannot understand the wisdom of the macro-cosmos based on our own human sensory and rational experiences. Therefore, we should not measure and judge people and things according to our intelligence and past experiences. We should focus on cultivating our body, mind and soul for clarity, purity and emptiness and not question macro-cosmic wisdom with our limited human perspectives, but rather choose to have faith in miracles. Counter to common belief, these miracles can include disasters, not only so called 'good' miracles. To only believe in good miracles is again falling into our ordinary mode of thinking. In order to enter the big Dao, we should set ourselves free from all the existing concepts and modes of thinking.

When we incorporate Dan practice into each and every moment of our everyday lives (i.e. being consciously aware of each thought and each action) the warning that disasters bring create a drive for positive change. Crises then become an opportunity and motivation for human beings to become transformed and enter into higher dimensional levels.

## Appendix A – Western Alchemy

Schools of mysticism had long traditions in ancient Egypt, Greece and Rome and were the Western equivalent of the Chinese concepts of internal alchemy. They knew that there is a blueprint embodied in human spirituality and the method to restart and unfold this blueprint is through alchemy - internal alchemy.

This alchemy uses the human body as the experimental laboratory. It is a technique that through controlling one's own physical energy field, one can gain understanding and control of the invisible energy field. It is about how to consciously manage the interactions between your personal Qi field and energy fields in your environment. It starts with self-awareness and consciousness toward cultivating super-energy receptiveness and on until eventually entering the spiritual world. The secret of all these masters is invariably to 'live in the present moment'.

The Western alchemists of the $12^{th}$ and $13^{th}$ centuries practiced secret keeping, stillness and quietness, and concentrated power of consciousness to transform energy into materials and vice versa. This in turn enabled the transformation of time and space itself. They developed a state of high frequency light in order to see the creator (that they referred to as God) in that light. All kinds of miracles would occur in the extremely high fire and heat frequencies. From these practices they realised that a person must let go of the heavy burdens of the past so that he or she can reach a moment of emptiness where the bright white light of the higher frequency field appears. When entering this field and being surrounded by this light, the light melted away any diseases and, in so doing, returned them to their origins. The origins of all diseases are the low and heavy 'iron and lead' impure energy fields. The purpose of human life is to learn how to smelt away these impurities and enter the strong energy field of high frequency golden light, or silver light, thus elevating the level of the energy fields of human beings as a whole.

I began to learn about the Western tradition of 'immortal practice' from Dr. Caroline Myss. Caroline is well versed in American military and political history but has her doctorate in theology, specialising in the study of Western religions. She used to work as a reporter, and as a co-owner of a publishing house in America. Needless to say, she is an extremely proficient writer and eloquent speaker. She keeps very close ties with nuns and was educated in Catholic schools for more than 20 years of her life. Her ability for remotely observing, diagnosing and treating has been studied by the famous American medical professional Dr. Norm Sheely, PhD. He has cooperated with her in a clinic type setting for over 20 years. She has the reputation for being one of the most accurate medical intuitives in diagnosis and treatment.

She started out by giving one to one healing and went on to become a teacher of energy medicine which is focused on how to apply your knowledge of your own mentality and its relationship to your health in daily life. She applies the yogic traditional theory of the seven chakras (energy centres) to explain the processes and practices of body and mind optimisation. She has provided a very clear description between the relationships of Western history and theology and the tradition of spiritual practice, which qualifies her as one of the most important heirs and spokespersons for Western alchemy in the contemporary world.

**The following summary is based on my understanding of her teachings of Western alchemy:**

There are mainly two schools of Western alchemy, namely the 'small mystics' and the 'big mystics'. The commonality shared by the two schools is 'secret keeping', i.e. it is forbidden to talk about the practices of quietness and emptiness, because it will lead to the leakage of Qi.

The 'small mystics' give particular attention to the stability of the physical world provided by the five senses, and emphasise logic. They insisted on persistent and regular daily practices corresponding to the daily cycles and regularities of the cosmic Qi field. For instance, they emphasised the importance of regular lifestyle routines. They tried to keep the stability of their bodies and minds as a part of every single moment of their daily lives. For them, it was a kind of correspondence between nature and the human body accomplished through linking the human body's magnetic field with the cosmic magnetic field. It was very much like the Daoist's Zi-Wu-Mao-You Practice (four times daily), through maintaining a regular routine to help stabilise the magnetic field of the human body.

The 'big mystics' practiced inner strength to reach a level where they could control their own energy fields to be able to transform their bodies. At the same time they could generate the ability to control the surrounding world, its time, space and speed. Their practice taught the ability to control the external energy field and the form of the physical world.

For example, Padre Pio, was a Cappuchin Priest of San Giovanni Rotondo. Now deemed a saint by the Vatican, Saint Pio was a contemporary monk of the $20^{th}$ century and did amazing work in his lifetime. He was known to have received the five wounds of Christ (stigmata), have the ability to heal the sick and be blessed with the ability of bi-location. There is a record in the US Pentagon of an occasion during the Second World War when the US military were preparing to bomb the small town of San Giovanni Rotondo as they expected to find Nazis there. A townsman went to Saint Pio and asked him to do something. The Nazis never came to the town but the US air force did not know this and when they were in mid-flight en route to this small Italian town all the pilots recorded seeing a monk in the sky with stigmata hands. This monk, who was flying in mid-air, asked them to turn back. So each pilot turned from their course, dropped their bombs over empty fields (as they were not allowed to return to base with armed explosives) and, on their return, reported to their superiors what they had each seen.

**Some Important Points Regarding Western Alchemy**

1. The knowledge, mastery, and control of invisible energy is key. Under ordinary circumstances, the majority of your energy is not in present time, i.e. not in the same location that your body occupies at that moment. For instance, as you read this book, you are likely not one hundred percent here and present while reading it. The essence of alchemy is to have a total knowing of where your energy field is, including your field of consciousness, i.e. where you are and what you are doing. All of you! Is it in the past? Or gone to visit a friend's home? Perhaps dwelling on a difficult situation or emotional complication? One needs to know where their consciousness has gone or where it is lost, as well as how to get it back.

   When you are trying to recollect and heal your problems by yourself, you are sitting here, but your soul is not in your body. This dispersed energy and scattered Qi will cause a low energy field. Chinese medicine describes it as 'weak Qi'. To be in a state of weak Qi one cannot transform or get rid of the origins of any disease. Both big and small mystics in Western alchemy, in general, are concerned with transforming human energy into materials and vice versa, through spiritual practices. Turning the heavy to light; changing from a living form which is exclusively manipulated by external fate to an active living being which has significant free will.

2. From the above point, it can be concluded that the purpose of life is alchemy, i.e. humans come to the Earth in order to practice, and a meaningful human life is an ongoing process of obtaining a golden heart.

3. The focus of ancient Roman and Greek alchemy was based on the technique of managing one's own energy and consciousness field and metaphorically 'melting one's heavy lead' (the low energy field which hinders human evolution is represented as lead in this case) and turning it into gold (the resultant high energy field). This method was based on eight experimental laboratories associated with the human body to facilitate the smelting practice in accordance with each laboratory's function. These laboratories corresponded with the chakras of yogic tradition.

The first, second and third chakras required, according to these alchemists, processes of smelting raw materials of lead and iron that were gained through experiences with people and events in society, family and nature. A person needed to practice discipline, tenacity, and experience these processes through their actions in the physical world. Through the process of normal daily life and rituals the aim of the practice was to drag one's soul back into one's body, i.e. to place the energy of one's spirit back within the physical body. But if this doesn't happen, often there is a separation of ideas (thoughts) and actions. This in itself is a phenomenon where spiritual energy and body energy fail to converge and are therefore unable to manifest.

**Chakras and Pyramids Diagram**

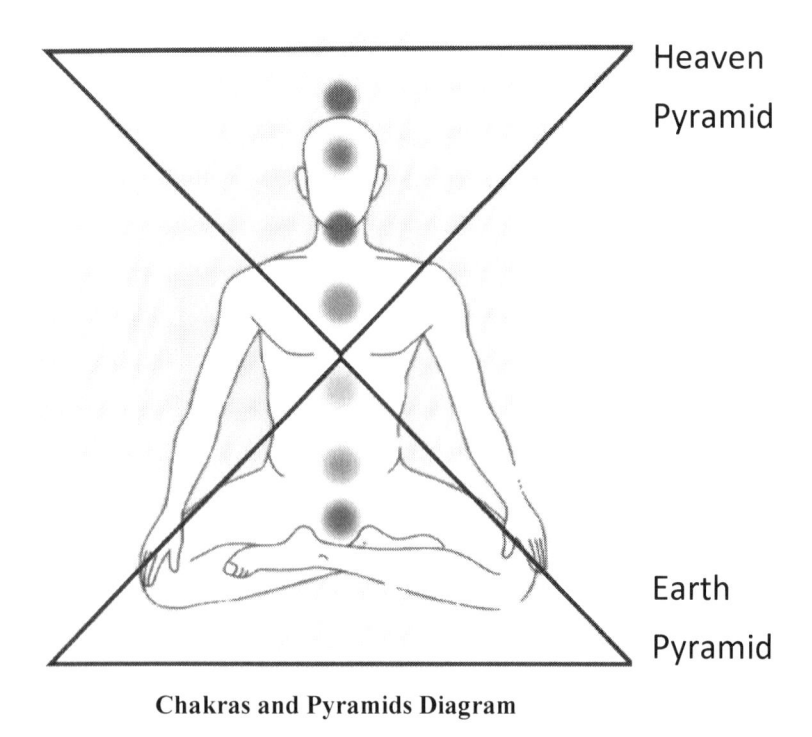

These first three chakras, which are below the solar plexus are called the physical energy fields, and are related to nature, family, one's own self, religion, nationality and the military.

In the fourth and fifth chakras, the task is to smelt matter into energy. It is based on unconditional love of oneself, and then goes beyond self-love to the love of others. It is the opening of one's heart and the forgiveness and tolerance of others' problems. These kinds of expressions of genuine courage and willpower are very close to the qualities of immortals and can lead to the healing of physical illnesses.

In the realm of the sixth to seventh chakras one enters the energy arena of the heart and soul, i.e. one's own spirit and the external spiritual fields of the immortals. The energy field of the human body seeks to gravitate toward a truthful world and the more truthful, the higher the frequencies and the higher the levels that are obtained.

The eighth chakra is a frequency field that is formless and has its own characteristics that can be termed as being archetypal in nature. This field is set up before birth, and is referred to by some as a spiritual contract with the immortal world prior to reincarnating. Everybody on average has twelve main archetypes. These are associated with human beings to act as a support system for each individual's energy field.

There are four basic archetypes that are possessed by everybody, namely the prostitute, child, victim, and saboteur. In one's lifetime, there are two developmental tendencies, i.e. to succeed in practice leading to the enhancement of your spiritual energy, or to fail in practice leading to the destruction of your spiritual energy. For instance, the archetype of the prostitute doesn't just relate to the professional prostitute who sells their body in exchange for money, but also relates to the cultured woman who forces themselves into an unhappy marriage for the sole reason of obtaining financial security from their husband. It also applies to men when they are engaged in jobs and professions they are unhappy doing, but remain there solely for the sake of the salary or security it provides. These are all manifestations of the prostitute archetype, (i.e. to go against one's own feelings of the heart and thus do things solely for material existence).

Likewise, everybody has some traits of the saboteur archetype. An example is when people do not speak the truth in a certain situation, even though they know deep down that speaking the truth would be good for their wellbeing. Another example is where people know that doing exercise first thing in the morning will be good for their health, but don't do anything about it. They'll just remain doing what they've always done and simply make 'logical' excuses as to why they're not doing what they know will be good for them.

The child archetype is about learning how to turn a child that has a lack of any sense of security and has a total dependence on others, into someone that can take responsibility for themselves to become one that is true to themselves and to others, and is completely free from fear. In Chinese, we often compliment a person with the phrase 'to have a red child's heart', meaning an adult who is very truthful and honest but at the same time is very experienced and has a mature nature in real life.

If you haven't resolved the necessary issues in chakra levels 1-3 or 4-5 at a young age - specifically the ability to turn spiritual energy into material and then material back into energy - then your eighth chakra and the four archetypes will not transform into their ideal states. Once you've reached your late thirties and early forties this can often manifest as a 'mid-age crisis'. On the contrary however, if you have laid out a good foundation in the earlier stages of life, you will evolve from being a victim to a victor. You can elevate every archetype to a higher Qi field, so that you can continue your further evolution with less risks and pain. If the four archetypes are still unresolved though, it means one has more work to do, more impurities have to be smelted. In this case, more painful experiences will be involved. Actually, the process of smelting is very simple. As long as mind and body are in harmony (with the spirit in the body), focusing consciousness on the problem will lead to it being smelted right away. A person with a very strong energy field will have no fear; therefore, one thought will immediately turn and dissolve any issue into a higher frequency light. God is in the light. If one does not eradicate the heavy iron and lead (i.e. the past, selfishness, desires etc), there will be many obstacles to pass before one can gain the Dan.

This is why we often observe the middle age crisis phenomenon at about the age of 40. At 40, if a person is still exhibiting the prostitute archetype, their inner self will be very discontented. Half their life has passed, but they are still doing things they don't want to do, i.e. selling their soul for security and survival. This is a state where ones true self is masked and twisted and where the body, mind and soul have not become the true masters. By this time, the body will most likely have contracted some form of illness and there will be serious warning signs, or ones current lifestyle and environment that they have sold their soul for will experience a great change and shift. These are all natural phenomena to increase the smelting heat when the soul and spirit sense the urgency for elevation. You have to follow the lead by changing your way of living and thinking, and give up the ties to the past.

Making up your twelve main archetypes are the four basic ones that everyone shares and then there are eight different archetypes that people have which will vary from one person to the next. Some examples of these archetypes include the teacher, hero, martyr, fool, queen, engineer, wizard, prophet, princess, doctor, and so on.

For instance, if a person with a hero archetype were to take a role in a play, he would fit best the hero role. He would be more suited to and convincing in this role. If he was to take the role of a fool however, and he didn't possess this archetype, it would not be very convincing to others or to him or herself. These archetypes are particular energies that are individual and therefore specific to each individual. I will not go into detail here since there are so many energy types and sub types.

The alchemy itself is to obtain a conscious understanding of all these energy systems (chakras and archetypes). With this knowledge a person will become able to smelt away their problems in life, and willingly and happily increase heat and control the heat to reach an optimal state. They will eventually become very familiar with their own archetypes and characteristics so that they can maximise the utilisation of their own Qi field.

At the same time, they will be able to decode the secret password at the eighth chakra state. That is, to become fully aware of the spiritual contract agreed between themselves and the immortal world before they came to Earth.

During these processes of real life experiences and developing a realisation of one's own Qi and magnetic energy field, and the understanding of one's contract with the immortals, a person will truly and fully start to live in the present moment. They will have totally dissolved the ego and turned heavy to light and darkness to brightness. Many experiences deemed 'extraordinary' by others will then simply become ordinary. The breadth and speed of a person's practice of the extraordinary will be related to their original system setup, as well as the degree of stillness that they have developed within themselves in terms of both length and depth.

## Chakras in Relation to Heaven, Human and Earth

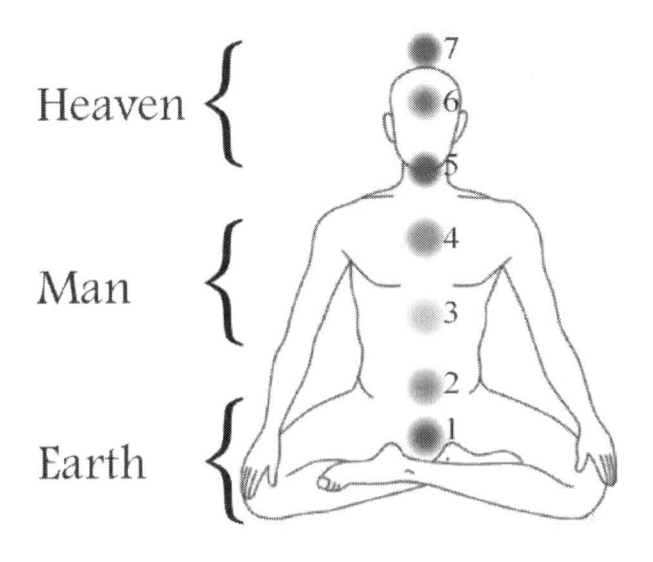

Heaven {

Man {

Earth {

**Seventh Chakra** - Resides above the head. Relates to Heaven, Spirit, the immortal world, soul family, complete perfection

**Sixth Chakra** - This is the energy area of the mind and soul of the spirit and resides behind the eyes. Clarity, inner wisdom, focus and concentration.

**Fifth Chakra** - Resides in the area of the throat. Expression of courage and willpower. How to use one's own willpower to deal with the external world. To be truthful is an expression of willpower. One must respect and acknowledge one's own spirit.

**Fourth Chakra** – Resides in the area of the heart. Compassionate, non-language guidance comes from the heart. Opening the heart to love both forgives and tolerates other people's problems.

**Third Chakra** - Resides below the solar plexus. Trustworthiness, reliability, self-awareness, intuition, confidence and self-improvement. Relationship to oneself and one's body.

**Second Chakra** – Is located in the lower abdomen and relates to creativity, instinct, addiction, sex, money, abortion, desire to control and be controlled, creativity, weapons (military), a sense of guilt will affect this chakra.

**First Chakra** - Resides at the root of your spine and relates to the Earth, root, tribes, religions, nationalities, collective consciousness, Karma, revenge, discipline, loyalty, tenacity, persistence in daily practices. If there is conflict within one's own family or country this chakra will be affected. If the first chakra is weak then a person is more susceptible to infectious diseases.

The chakra system is a continual flow system of Qi and vibration. **To be able to cultivate and remain in a high vibrational frequency, a person needs to be truthful to themselves and learn to live in the present moment.**

# Appendix B – Mountain Skills in Nine Parts

## Part One - Moving Practice (also called Daoyin Practice in ancient times)

a) Physical exercise.
b) Moving practice that imitates animal motions (e.g. Hua Tuo five animal play).
c) Self-healing and protection methods.
d) Guiding the Qi motion of the meridians.

## Part Two - Still Practice (also called the 'Three Degrees Of Spiritual Practice' in ancient times)

a) To practice the human heart. This is to be able to recognise higher spirits when the mind and heart is still and quiet. The mind and heart will become still and quiet when you become less distracted by desire; then the divine spirit will become clear.
b) To practice the heavenly heart. This is to fulfil the Yin spirit, so that you are able to see the divine truth while in an empty state and are able to see the shape and the form of both the internal and external.
c) To practice the Daoist heart. This is to reveal the Yang spirit, so that you can travel freely in all of the dimensions

of the cosmos and therefore in and out of the three dimensions of Earthly reality.

The method of practicing the heart is the important pathway to reach the truth of the cosmos. It involves mostly sitting in Lotus posture meditations.

## Part Three - Qi Gong Breathing

**There are three types:**

a) Qi Gong 气: natural and cosmic breathing. Breathing in fresh Qi and breathing out toxic Qi in order to absorb the essence of Heaven and Earth and thus nourish the human body.

b) Qi Gong 炁: the cosmos' blueprint of the human body. Consolidate and nurture your original Jing, Qi and Shen by moving the Qi of the five organs in order to unblock the meridians.

c) Qi Gong 氮: the secret practices of the immortals. Arrange the Qi field by setting up an array to dismantle harmful Qi in order to cultivate peace and maintain good health.

## Part Four - External Alchemy: take medicine orally as an external support

a) Food – use food to nourish and cure.
b) Medicine –
    i. Treatment of disease.
    ii. To assist during certain stages of practice.
    iii. To assist the practice of special skills.

c) Alchemy (Dan) – used in higher level practices to eliminate poisons through the taking of poison.

## Part Five - Home Skills

There are twelve chapters in this section that include family life, the upbringing of children, hygiene, housing, feng shui etc

## Part Six - Internal Alchemy

Using the physical body to cultivate and return Dan:

a) Cultivate Dan: Using the lower, middle and upper Dantian as the furnace. Through cultivating the essence as the basic material (medicine), the consciousness as the fire (motor) and the spirit as the master, the essence, Qi and spirit will become an inseparable entity of Dan. Dan is stored in the Tian (central energy cavity), and hence is called the Dantian.

b) Return Dan: The route of Dan returning is the practice of the human body corresponding with the orbits of celestial bodies. These were called cosmic orbits in ancient times and include:
   i. The practice of the human body corresponding with one rotation of the Earth (24 hours) is called the Mao-You orbit cycle.
   ii. The practice of the human body corresponding with the moon's rotating cycle around the Earth is called the small orbit cycle.

iii. The practice of the human body corresponding with the Earth's rotating cycle around the sun (365 days) is called the big orbit cycle.

*Note: There are different levels of orbit cycles: the meridian orbit cycle, collaterals orbit cycle & the Dan pathway orbit cycle.*

c) Golden Dan: Dan that becomes one with heaven, Earth, the sun and the moon, leading the body to turn into an imperishable diamond.

## Part Seven - Talismans

This is a type of symbol that is a mixture of a picture and a written character. It is a method of communication which supports an information exchange between different cosmic worlds. Only talismans that are used by people who have a high energy vibration can hold any kind of real power and effect.

## Part Eight - Mantras

This is the same as praying. It is a series of syllables or words people recite either aloud or in the mind when they are practicing. It is a demonstration of sincerity when praying to an external power for help.

## **Part Nine - Array**

This is a method whereby the human body practices with celestial bodies. Practitioners set up and walk on arrays that are patterned according to certain celestial constellations, while using certain mantras that relate the two together thus allowing the human body and celestial body to vibrate at the same frequency. It can be a cost-effective method in spiritual practices and the treatment of diseases.

# About the Author

### Dr Bisong Guo

Dr Guo was born in China. She studied Western Medicine at Fuzhou Medical School before specialising in Classical Chinese Medicine (CCM). She is a Qi Gong master, having studied for over three decades with Buddhist Qi Gong masters and Daoist monks in remote mountainous regions of China.

Dr Guo has lectured on Daoism and Chinese Medicine extensively in the UK, continental Europe, Australia and the USA and still travels widely overseas conducting seminars and workshops and teaching Qi Gong.

She is the founding director of The Shen Foundation and the Classical Chinese Medicine Society, both of which are dedicated to the healing and transformation of humanity.

As an executive member and UK Ambassador for the World Federation of Acupuncture-Moxibustion Societies (WFAS), Dr Guo is currently collaborating with the World Health Organisation (WHO) for further development of CCM.

She is also involved in health and wellbeing leadership training, international cultural exchange projects and in the development of innovation in community healthcare including the design and implementation of digital health networks. Deeply concerned with the welfare of the planet, she is engaged with climate change and sustainability issues, including local movements such as Transition Town Forres, and the international disaster prevention initiative, the Hanwang Forum.

Dr. Guo is the author of 'Listen to Your Body – the Wisdom of the Dao' (co-authored with Dr Andrew Powell), with editions in English, Thai, Italian and Chinese. Other publications in TCM journals include:

- Guo, B. (1996) Applying the Method of Emptying the Mind Whilst Filling the Abdomen to Enhance the Effect of Acupuncture in Clinical Practice. Journal of Chinese Medicine, 52: 22-23.

- Guo, B. (1994) Introducing Qi Gong: Turn back the clock and rejuvenate. Journal of Chinese Medicine, 45: 14-17.

www.shenfoundation.net
www.classicalchinesemedicine.co.uk

Printed in Great Britain
by Amazon